Jews and Muslims in the White Supremacist Conspiratorial Imagination

Jews and Muslims in the White Supremacist Conspiratorial Imagination explores how Jews and Muslims are stigmatized and endangered by the same conspiratorial template.

Supremacists imagine that Jews and Muslims secretly strive to replace white, European civilization with an unspeakable tyranny. The authors, a Jew and a Muslim, analyze the nature of the conspiracism that targets their communities. They historicize the supremacist conspiratorial imagination, narrating the paranoia on a continuum, from modernity to the postmodern. They begin with the texts of modernity, following them through to the dark areas of the Internet and examining their violent denouement in synagogues and mosques. The book investigates the classic text *The Protocols of the Elders of Zion* and neoclassic variations such as QAnon. It turns to Islamophobic responses to 9/11 such as paranoia regarding the Muslim Brotherhood and the doppelgänger of *The Protocols*, namely *The Project*. The authors conclude by questioning how "ordinary" people, prompted by paranoia and recognition hunger, resort to violence and murder. Admittedly, the authors are not certain—certainty is for conspiracists. But they may have a piece of the puzzle.

This book will be of interest to students and scholars of conspiracy theories, antisemitism, Judeophobia, Islamophobia, political science, history, philosophy, psychology, sociology, and criminology.

Ron Hirschbein is Emeritus Professor of Philosophy at California State University, Chico, USA, where he created and headed the Peace Institute. He also served as Visiting Professor at the University of California campuses in Berkeley and San Diego, and at the United Nations University in Austria.

Amin Asfari is Associate Professor and Chair of the Department of Criminology in the School for Professional Advancement at Regis University, USA.

Conspiracy Theories

Series Editors: Peter Knight, *University of Manchester,* and **Michael Butter**, *University of Tübingen.*

Conspiracy theories have a long history and exist in all modern societies. However, their visibility and significance are increasing today. Conspiracy theories can no longer be simply dismissed as the product of a pathological mind-set located on the political margins.

This series provides a nuanced and scholarly approach to this most contentious of subjects. It draws on a range of disciplinary perspectives including political science, sociology, history, media and cultural studies, area studies and behavioural sciences. Issues covered include the psychology of conspiracy theories, changes in conspiratorial thinking over time, the role of the Internet, regional and political variations and the social and political impact of conspiracy theories.

The series will include edited collections, single-authored monographs and short-form books.

Jews and Muslims in the White Supremacist Conspiratorial Imagination

Ron Hirschbein and Amin Asfari

Routledge
Taylor & Francis Group
LONDON AND NEW YORK

First published 2023
by Routledge
4 Park Square, Milton Park, Abingdon, Oxon OX14 4RN

and by Routledge
605 Third Avenue, New York, NY 10158

Routledge is an imprint of the Taylor & Francis Group, an informa business

British Library Cataloguing-in-Publication Data
A catalogue record for this book is available from the British Library

ISBN: 978-1-032-07481-8 (hbk)
ISBN: 978-1-032-07607-2 (pbk)
ISBN: 978-1-003-20789-4 (ebk)

DOI: 10.4324/9781003207894

Typeset in Times New Roman
by Deanta Global Publishing Services, Chennai, India

Credo quia absurdum[1]

---

1 "I believe because it is absurd": Profession of faith attributed to early Church Fathers.

Contents

Dedication and Acknowledgments

Ron dedicates this study to his ancestors who perished in the Holocaust, and to the joy he derives from his children, Michelle and Jonah. He'd be remiss not to acknowledge his wife: Lee's encouragement enabled him to think clearly while immersed in the interstices of conspiracism.

Routledge editor Hannah Rich's patience, suggestions, and good nature facilitated the writing.

We're indebted to Dr Reza Zia-Ebrahimi for his encouragement and adroit criticism.

Amin dedicates this work to the Three Winners, Deah Barakat, Yusur and Razan Mohammad Abu-Salha, and all those slain by white supremacist terrorists.

To my children, Yusuf, Ayah, and Adam: May you benefit from this work and may it move you to be a force for good. To my life partner Vasilica: Your candor and encouragement through this process were immensely valuable, even in the darkest of moments.

Finally, I would like to acknowledge Hannah Rich, our editor, for her guidance throughout this project. I also thank Emily Bergen for her assistance in collecting the research materials.

Preface

Are we living in a surreal comic? Long ago, in a galaxy far away, conspiracists were a laughingstock—oddball cranks lost in a world of their own. We still encounter them in occasional *New Yorker* cartoons when a wizened old man prophesizes impending doom. The poet Berthold Brecht was right: "He who laughs last hasn't heard the terrible news." Those who watched the storming of the Capitol saw the terrible news in the person of the "QAnon Shaman": Looking like a discarded caricature found on the drawing room floor of a Marvel Comics studio, he desecrated the hallowed corridors. But, like other conspiracists, was he fanatically dedicated to a cause or suffering from insufferable recognition hunger? Perhaps both? Did he know himself?[1]

No wonder we almost long those bygone days when conspiracism was not at once bizarre, contagious, and terrifying. Not too long ago, when our parents skimmed the morning paper, sagas of conspiracies evoked a smile or a sneer. They chuckled when then-Senator Nixon uncovered evidence of Alger Hiss' Communist conspiratorial schemes in a pumpkin patch. The conspiracists of yesteryear were intrigued by tales of space aliens secreted at Area 51. No worries: Like a trusted physician, the aliens did no harm. The fun stopped when Senator Joseph McCarthy—relying upon bullying and innuendo—uncovered commies everywhere, even in the Bureau of Fish and Game; however, the witch-hunt had an expiration date—his colleagues censured his unseemly conduct. Not to be outdone, the John Birch Society discovered that President Eisenhower was a tool of the Communist conspiracy, even so the republic prevailed.

Conspiracism is no longer funny. It has gone high tech. Times have changed; the Red Scare is passé. (As we'll see, Frank Gaffney, Jr., a former promoter of the Red Scare, has moved on to the Green Scare—Islamophobia.) True, predictable beyond banality, rightwing politicians can't break the habit of smearing opponents as Communists. However, such tried and untrue calumny hardly merits a yawn—just another tiresome rerun of bygone political smears—a dud.

It's difficult to capture a distracted public's attention these days. Candidate Trump tried to drop a bombshell when he accused Hillary Clinton of clandestine meetings with international bankers to plot the destruction of United States sovereignty—echoes of the gospel of anti-semitism, *The Protocols of the Elders of Zion.* But such a classic con-spiratorial smear only prompted a few editorial denunciations—it didn't stick. (Not that antisemitism is taboo—it just required better branding and packaging.) White supremacists know how to market; they know that antisemitism unadorned no longer grabs attention; international bankers are a rather dull lot. White supremacist conspiracism needs accelerants—"bombshells."

Bombshells blast open grotesque conspiracies in three ways: pornogra-phy, science fiction, and the supernatural. Such conspiracism went off the rails with Trump's presidency. He was glad that QAnon conspiracists liked him; their affection did not go unrequited. In the unlikely event you haven't heard, QAnon cast Trump in his bravura role—a messianic redeemer. Hillary seems boring, but don't be deceived: In the world according to QAnon she leads a secret life in a bacchanal of debauchery that would repulse the Marquis de Sade. But don't assume that Hillary alone pulls the strings. As always, Jews reappear—along with Satan: A cabal of "globalists" headed by the likes of the Rothschilds and Soros—call the shots.

The cabal murders those who have the goods on Hillary—the least of their crimes. Repackaging ancient Jewish Blood Libels, we learn that Hillary and her minions (joined by au currant villains) conspire with other pedophiles and Satan worshippers to kidnap children and drink their blood. Satanic rites are so well-hidden that they could not be discovered by a conspiracist vigilante at the Comet Pizza Restaurant raid—proof positive of their diabolical cunning.

Conspiracists simply cannot imagine abandoning their fantasies: The search for evildoers remains thrilling—and dangerous. Life would be unbearably dull indeed if they didn't somehow find themselves in a Dan Brown novel ferreting out cryptic clues and connecting the dots. For the conspiracist, the terrible has already happened. Even so, there is hope: For it is written that Trump—the spear and shield of QAnon—will usher in the apocalypse, *The Storm,* that will destroy Hillary and her minions.

It takes a bombshell to capture our attention. How much does it exag-gerate to suggest that conspiracists, like others in the overdeveloped world, suffer from (or rather revel in) a collective attention deficit disorder? (This age of spectacles and commodities overwhelms with irresistible demands for our attention—just Google "hyperactivity" as you check your phone for the nth time today.) No wonder the insatiable conspiracist appetite craves more than the single bite of tantalizing conspiracies. Not surprisingly, the pandemic fomented infectious enthusiasm for a panoply of conspiracies old and new.

Trump exhorted the faithful to watch Dr. Stella Immanuel's videos: The good doctor pleased the president by mocking masking and by prescribing his favored malaria drug. But it will not do to merely put one's faith in better living through chemistry—grabbing attention demands more—much more! These latter-days unworldly visages arise in the conspiracists' hyperactive imaginations—attention must be paid to supernatural intrigues, for indeed, the devil reappears in the conspiracist imagination. Dr. Immanuel warns that demons have their way with us in our dreams—now *that's* interesting. (Ron wouldn't mind the encounters; he just wishes the demons would leave his prostate alone.)

It is difficult to think of a conspiracist who merely embraces a single conspiracy. Newly elected Representative Marjorie Taylor Greene endorsed much of the QAnon canon and much else. Like most conspiracists she posts on the Internet—the world's greatest propaganda machine—to broadcast her revelations far and wide. Among her revelations: 9/11 was an inside job, and, like the Las Vegas murders, the Parkland school shooting was a hoax. Not surprisingly, she traffics in antisemitism and Islamophobia. Of course, the cliched antisemitic canards are no longer bombshells—who wants to talk of Shylock when *Star Wars* is viewed in 3D?

Now Ron literally gagged in the smoke from the 2018 Paradise, California fire—the worst in the state's history. Ms. Greene exploded a bombshell in her Facebook posting: In her cartoon imagination, Jew-operated space lasers (perhaps controlled by an Elder of Zion?) set the quaint foothill town aflame. (Or maybe the Rothschilds had an abiding interest in this piney, retirement community. But why this place and no other?)

Her Islamophobia isn't as imaginative. She merely recycled claims about a Muslim fifth-column plotting the destruction of American civilization as we know it. (No need to cite evidence. To reiterate, as Greene and other conspiracists know, diabolic conspiracies cleverly hide evidence of their malevolence.) She warned that Muslim jihadists dream of a planetary caliphate; however, until that day dawns, they conspire to impose Shira Law. No surprise to the representative: She already knew that President Obama and his top advisors are closet Muslims.

Living in this world of cartoon villains and heroes, there are many conspiracies to analyze—why focus upon Jews and Muslims? We obviously have a parochial interest, and unfortunately, we can list acts of white supremacist terror committed against our respective groups. Indeed, as we've already suggested, diverse conspiracies begin with a common denominator. These latter days it is difficult to think of conspiracism that doesn't default to paranoid fantasies about the secret, malevolent machinations of maligned Jews xiv *Preface*

and Muslims—the signature nemesis of the white supremacist imagination. To be sure, supremacists have no affection for Blacks and Orientals; indeed, non-Whites don't belong in their ethno-state. However, they seldom imagine these minorities conspiring against them. They're obsessed with Jews and Muslims. They imagine Jews and Muslims plotting to replace privileged European civilization with minorities who have no business occupying hallowed white spaces.

Supremacist conspiracism knows no borders; it is not just an American brand; many nationalities vie for "edgelord" status (infamy in Internet cant) on the conspiracists' go-to websites. We've witnessed diverse nationalities communicating on these sites in virtual 24/7 white supremacist rallies. (It is at once amusing and chilling to invoke pseudonyms in order to spy upon these networks to witness the gamesmanship as supremacists vie to become the most transgressive—much like delinquent teens vying to spray-paint the most offensive graffiti.) But once again with Brecht we lament, "Woe to the nation that needs heroes." And so we close by hazarding an account of conspiracists' taunting and challenging their anonymous brothers to live the dream: heroic journeys ending in arson and murder in our mosques and synagogues. And yet we have not given up hope. Finding solace in a more sanguine poet, Theodore Rothke, we would like to believe that "In a dark time the eye begins to see."

Note

1 The so-called QAnon Shaman (Jacob Chansley) became the face of the insurrection. He was diagnosed with several mental illnesses; nevertheless, he was sentenced to 41 months in prison for a variety of violations.

Introduction
White Lives Matter—More!

This collaboration between a Jew and Muslim reveals we're both stigmatized and endangered by the same conspiratorial fantasy, an idée fixe: Conspiracists imagine that we Jews and Muslims have nothing better to do than to conspire to replace European civilization with a tyranny such that the world has never known—a Jewish monarchy or a Muslim caliphate. Either way, the white race is doomed—just ask the shooters who terrorize our synagogues and mosques. Consumed by a passion for high drama and acclaim, these white supremacists simply cannot abide the lackluster notion that we are ordinary people leading routine lives—the ordinary becomes other. The surge in white supremacist terror prompts our overarching concern: What's the fatal attraction of the conspiracism that finds its violent denouement in our houses of worship?

Conspiracists don't fret about real, exigent problems that demand calm, careful analysis: issues such as affordable healthcare, quality housing and education, let alone climate change.[1] (We can almost hear Homer Simpson groaning "booooring.") Nonexistent threats from Jews and Muslims unhinge the conspiracist from the constraints of reality and the burden of critical thought. We cannot imagine apocalyptic conspiracism without its signature histrionics—a passion for Manichean drama. Not known for their humility and restraint, conspiracists claim prophetic vision; they have seen the writing on the wall. Engrossed in a charade, they fancy themselves as crusaders on the frontlines of an impending apocalypse—the fate of their imagined race, if not the fate of the Earth, hangs in balance.

The World According to Richard Spencer

What *is* this white supremacy? Indeed, just who *is* white in the supremacist's imagination? It is tempting to dismiss, if not indict, such questions by recalling Einstein's admonition penned amid the ascendant nuclear threat: "Remember your humanity and forget the rest." However, such cosmopolitan humanism is anathema to supremacists who, hungering for recognition, treasure their imagined, special identities above all else— they fear that white lives *won't* matter. As political scientist Colin Flint explains:

> White racist activists must adopt a political identity of whiteness, the flimsy definition ... in modern culture poses a special challenge ... In both mainstream and white supremacist discourse, to be white is distinct from those marked as non-white, yet the distinguishing line placement has varied significantly in different times and places.[2]

The supremacists' embrace of "whiteness" is self-confessional—a revelation of narcissistic longings bereft of biologic fact and historical insight. Academics, as is our wont, recognize that social constructions such as "whiteness" are ambiguous and contested. However, supremacists have little appetite for self-reflection and academic controversy. Spencer is not plagued by uncertainty—no patience for overthinking the notion of whiteness. As he explains: "Any concept of identity could be knocked down if overanalyzed, and over analysis would only lead to inaction. I could just sit here masturbating in my own filth."[3] Supremacists cling to an identity of whiteness as if their immortal souls depend upon it. An indelible image of their whiteness—bestowed by the grace of God—is fixed in their imaginations.

Spencer (credited with coining the term "Alt Right" and pictured celebrating President Trump's 2016 victory with Sieg Heil salutes) imagines Europeans as *the* White Race. He mandates that: "The *Volksgeist* ... was that of white Christendom, a group with indistinct geographical borders, but roughly including European peoples, from Iberia to the Caucasus, who were Christian as of a few hundred years ago." And curiously, like other supremacists who celebrate Christianity, along with comrades born pure in race and spirit, Spencer excludes non-Christians, namely Jews. (Apparently, Jesus, Joseph, and Mary, and the Apostles don't belong in his imagined Christian ethno-state. Did Nietzsche's get it right? "There was only one Christian, and He died on the cross.")

Quiet modesty is not a supremacist virtue. What Freud called "The narcissism of minor group difference" stands out in stark relief. The sui generis white supremacist chooses his or her parents wisely and boasts of an ennobling heritage—one of a kind indeed! Celebrating his heritage, convicted murderer and arsonist John Earnest writes that: "It is not in my blood to be a coward. I am blessed by God for such a magnificent bloodline."[4] As we'll see, after celebrating his courageous heritage, he brags about setting fire to a mosque as the inhabitants slept, and game *on*! He vows to attain the highest kill score by murdering helpless Jewish worshippers in suburban San Diego. (He used a rifle; he would have preferred a flamethrower.)

He also claims to be a Christian who worships Jesus—a Jew not blessed by his imagined bloodline. Apparently, he and the other supremacists are not troubled by cognitive dissonance—a signature of conspiracy theory. We indict such contempt for reason as "cognitive insolence."

White supremacists have an exalted view of *their* rightful destiny, but what fate awaits others? Some are merely concerned with preserving, extending, and exalting white privilege. Others urge dominating, oppressing, and expelling—if not exterminating—perfidious inferiors. We're endangered by the latter—the John Earnests of the world: It is they who marched on Charlottesville and terrorized our mosques and synagogues. However, more pragmatic supremacists like Spencer, concerned with making a wider appeal, affect a genteel ethos—at least in public—their putative principles suit the occasion.

Dapper, well-spoken (given his graduate studies in the humanities), he argues that if Jews can have their ethno-state, why not Europeans? However, much to his chagrin, the Unite the Right rally in Charlottesville went awry and got bad press. Milo Yiannopoulos (a fellow supremacist) taped Spencer's outburst—a gran mal catharsis: an outburst that reveals Spencer's persona. "I am so mad. I am so fucking mad at these people. They don't do this to fucking me. We are going to fucking ritualistically humiliate them."[5]

To be sure, white supremacists have no affection for Asians and Blacks. However, by and large, they are not consumed by irrational fears that these minorities are plotting against them. The supremacist response to us is *phobic*: anxiety about an imagined, hidden cabal (globalists) conspiring to replace, if not exterminate, them *the* white race—"white genocide." This *"Replacement Theory"* reverberated through the streets of Charlottesville and echoes in the manifestos of supremacist terrorists obsessed with making a name for themselves. We're particularly concerned with replacement theorists such as John Earnest, Robert Bowers, and Brenton Tarrant. The deranged acts of these mass murderers have not discredited the theory. On the contrary, it is promulgated on Fox News and echoed in the halls of Congress. In an article entitled "How the ugly, racist White 'replacement theory' came to Congress," CNN political analyst, Chris Cillizza reveals:

> Pennsylvania Republican Rep. Scott Perry used a House Foreign Affairs Committee ... to spread the ugly, racist theory that "native

born [read White] Americans are being purposely replaced by immigrants …. to permanently transform the landscape of this very nation."

Cillizza goes on to explain that various theorists blame the Jews (the conspiracists' default position) working in concert with liberal politicians. Such conspiracism is no longer "the stuff of internet fever swamps." He reminds the reader that other representatives such as Steve King share Perry's apprehension. King is quoted as admonishing: "We can't restore our civilization with somebody else's babies."[6]

Curiously, in the supremacist imagination, we Jews and Muslims are lesser beings. Nevertheless—perhaps in league with Satan—we possess uncanny powers to undermine, if not destroy, God's finest creation—*the white race*. Somehow the *ubermensch* imagines himself victimized by the malevolent machinations of his inferiors.

Of course, white supremacists never tire of extolling their superior racial identity and entitlement. Such narcissism is simply "racial realism" in their lexicon; the implications are disturbing. Biology being destiny, it is a crime against nature—if not the Almighty—unless whites prevail and rule. But upon whom should white privilege be bestowed? At times, Southern and Eastern Europeans (even the Irish) were excluded from the fold; these latter-days they qualify as "honorary whites." But what of Jews and Muslims who appear Caucasian? That Jews pass as white is further proof of their cunning. (It may also be due to the research that reveals the European heritage of Ashkenazi Jews.[7]) Even so, according to certain notable supremacists, a careful observer—such as Hitler's phrenologists—can differentiate Jews from the Master Race. Phrenology proved to be an inexact science.

The Perfect Aryan Child

As Hitler consolidated power, Nazi propagandists extolled the aesthetics and the virtues of the imagined Aryan Race. Propaganda Minister Joseph Goebbels sponsored a beauty contest to discover "the perfect Aryan child." In 1934 a young Latvian couple migrated to Berlin and had a portrait taken of their beguiling child. Their photographer couldn't resist the temptation to enter the portrait in the contest. The child of these Latvian Jews won. Her "photo was everywhere. It first adorned a Nazi magazine … and then was later splashed across postcards and storefronts … the perfect Aryan."[8]

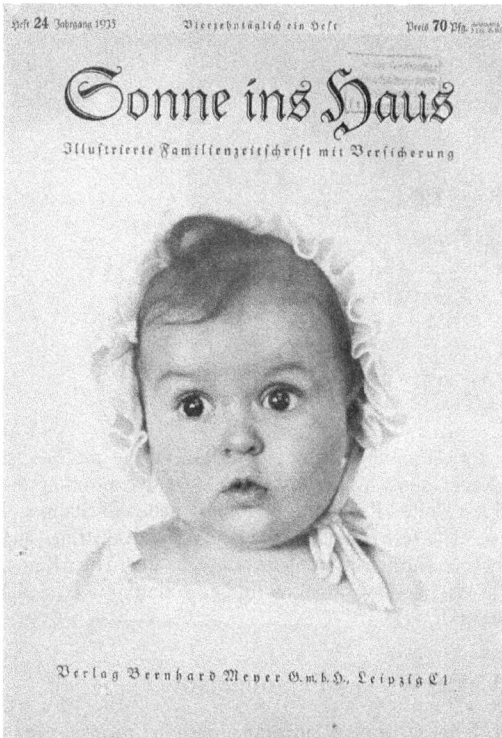

Figure 0.1 Front cover photograph of Hessy Levinsons, the winner of the most beautiful Aryan baby contest—whose promoters never discovered her Jewish ancestry, published on the cover of a Nazi magazine. Source: "Sonne ins Haus" magazine (Life time: Defunct Nazi magazine), Public domain, via Wikimedia Commons January 1935: Germany (https://commons.wikimedia.org/wiki/File:Hessy_Levinsons_Taft.jpg).

The Abstract Jew

Not surprisingly, there's a marked contrast between the diverse array of individual Jews and the imagined abstract Jew. No wonder Hitler required Jews to wear yellow stars to shape-shift the ordinary to the other. Latter-day white supremacists trolling the Internet rely upon triple brackets to identify Jews like (((Hirschbein))). With the exception, perhaps of George Soros (who looks like an ordinary fellow seen on a park bench feeding pigeons) the conspiracists rarely picture actual Jews. Their "Jew" becomes an imaginative villainous and controlling abstraction, a meme.

Figure 0.2 A Serbian poster for an exhibition in 1941–1942 during the Fascist regime of Milan Nedic, showing the Jews and Masons controlling the Soviet Union and the United Kingdom, with marionettes of Stalin and Churchill. Caption: "The Jew is holding the strings. Whose strings and how? He'll answer you. The anti-masonic exhibit." Source: Third Reich, Public domain, via Wikimedia Commons (https://commons.wikimedia.org/wiki/File:Posters11.jpg).

It's an Uncanny World After All—A Personal Note

Our middle-class academic lives are rather ordinary, perhaps more so than we'd like—we too have pangs of recognition hunger. However, since we've learned more about supremacist conspiracism than we care to know, we find ourselves at a paradoxical juncture—an uncanny space at once familiar, yet unnervingly strange—the irony doesn't escape us. Our respective histories are chronicles of exclusion and demonization marked by violent persecution. But for now, life remains rather placid and routine. We tread on familiar terrain: we don't feel like strangers in a strange land—not yet. Even so, there is foreboding—how could there not be after our deep immersion in the white supremacists' conspiratorial imagination brought to life in the Capitol insurrection? Does the insurrection foretell dark times? As novelist Stephen Marche writes: "The unimaginable has become everyday in America. Buffoonish mobs desecrating the US Capitol building, tear gas and tanks on the streets of Washington, DC, running battles between protestors and militias ...."[9]

The Rise of the Social Media

We give appropriate weight to the role of the social media in precipitating events that unnerve commentators such as Marche. Virulent conspiracism infects the body politic. This media, an imperium (perhaps *the* imperium) weaponizes social discourse and bestows anyone with an Internet connection an aura of credibility and an audience. As Mike Rothschild observes in his penetrating account of QAnon, it is difficult to overstate the role of the Internet in spreading conspiracism; how unlike the bad old days! As he explains:

> Before the Internet, believing in a conspiracy theory took work. You had to know which dank bookstore to patronize, and which gun show or truck stop was selling the hot new anti-Clinton video, or find the right shortwave radio broadcasts about UN stormtrooper invasions ... It made spreading these theories to the uninitiated more difficult.[10]

The isolation due to the ongoing pandemic, global demographic shifts caused by wars and climate change, and economic reshuffling, foment a virtually solipsistic existence ruled by an impoverished imagination bereft of the richness of reality. (Could it be that, shorn of its conspiratorial cloak, antisemitism and Islamophobia are merely venal prejudices repackaged for the postmodern Internet age?) Gazing into the pixilated haze, the addicted user succumbs to every fanaticism—the more absurd, the more believable. White nationalism, marked by Jew hatred and Islamophobia, ranks among the most pernicious. In-person dialogue, contact with other human beings, is for "normies." Transgressive memes—cringe-worthy icons of xenophobia seek denouement in livestreamed acts of hate. We're cast as super villains plotting to bring down Western civilization—quite an accomplishment for our negligible numbers. We seek to uncover the Internet virulence that distorts the white supremacist imagination and infects the body politic.

Our Candidate

Prior to offering glosses on each chapter, we wish to nominate an anonymous, albeit ideal, candidate for recruitment to white supremacist conspiracism. Writing in the *Atlantic*, journalists Kaufman, Weigel, and Tsang scanned the social media and recount the lamentation of a distraught young man—with a "proclivity to become bored easily."

> "Give me, a white man, a reason to live ... Should I get a hobby? ..." [A] fellow user had a suggestion; [it wasn't stamp collecting]: "Please write a concise book of only factual, indisputable information exposing the Jews ... and their long track record of pedophilia and perversion etc."[11]

We know not whether this distraught young man published or perished. We'll refer to him as Our Candidate and comment upon what each iteration of supremacist conspiracism offers those suffering terminal ennui. He might be an ideal recruit for QAnon: The deepest despair beckons the most soaring fantasy—"a dialectic of despair."

Chapter 1: Conspiracism—Modern and Postmodern

How shall we conceptualize the conspiracism that stigmatizes and endangers us? Fixed dictionary definitions fail to capture its evolving historical nature—its metamorphosis. Indeed, the overused term "conspiracy theory" often impedes conceptual analysis. Weaponized to disparage opponents, it's promiscuously applied—especially to those who depart from convention by indicting malevolence in high places. We hasten to add that, as the Tuskegee outrage illustrates, real conspiracies exist.

Striving for conceptual clarity, with Nietzsche we argue that concepts with a history cannot be defined—they must be narrated. Accordingly, subsequent chapters historicize the supremacist conspiratorial imagination—a project long overdue. We narrate the conspiracists' febrile imaginations on a continuum beginning with the tattered texts of modernity, follow them through the dark interstices of the postmodern Internet, and analyze their violent denouement in synagogues and mosques.

We view classical conspiracism theory through the fixed-focus lens of modernity: ostensibly a quest for certainty, but man does not live by cognition alone. Driven by religious zeal, theorists become smug theologians: neo-Gnostics, prophets privy to secret revelations—Jeremiads warn of a terrible evil to come. Keeping the faith, the conspiracist theologian yearns for a redemptive, cleansing apocalypse.

By way of contrast, postmodern conspiracism eschews grand theory and putative evidence in favor of transgressive entertainment. The sense of the sacred, endemic to classical conspiracy theory, let alone faith in the dawn of a glorious millennium, is for "normies." Akin to teenage delinquents scrawling offensive graffiti, postmodern conspiracists vie for the most cringe-worthy Internet posting. We witness this latter-day conspiracism through a kaleidoscope of the histrionic postmodern. Driven by insatiable recognition hunger, the postmodernist is an entertainer, not a prophet. Risible memes trump old-fashioned prophesy. Since, as communication theorist Neil Postman[12] recognized long ago, entertainment is the métier of American culture, Our Candidate might eschew theoretical ruminations in favor of conjuring transgressive memes—*the* path to latter-day recognition. We cannot imagine what the postmodern conspiracist would *not* do to gain recognition.[13] All this said, as we'll see, modern and postmodern conspiracism are not discrete entities. Chapter 1 analyzes the dialectic interplay between these conspiracist genres.

Chapter 2: Long Ago in a Prague Cemetery Far Away

Drilling down into the conspiratorial imagination, we find the fetid effluvia of *the* iconic antisemitic[14] fabrication, *The Protocols of the Learned Elders of Zion*.[15] We conceptualize the classic forgery in a Janus-like perspective—a conduit linking past, present, and future. Looking backward it absorbs the tried and untrue calumnies of the past. The forgery emerged amid the inchoate discontents of modernity instantiated in the abstract Jew—a race bent on destroying all that is sacred. Today, it offers true believers a ringside seat to the ongoing conspiracy. The Senior Elder, the sole spokesman, introduces himself—a bad first impression. He reveals he and his minions as cunning Jews scheming for imminent world domination by all means necessary. (Spoiler alert: It didn't happen.)

The *Protocols'* tattered texts may never be laid to rest. Like the vampires that emerged in the 19th-century imagination, the forgery will not die—it haunts latter-day darkness. Ancient libels are reincarnated in neoclassics (novels such as *The Turner Diaries*) and memeified on the postmodern Internet. We'd be remiss not to give dishonorable mention to QAnon.

Chapter 3: The Muslim Brotherhood(s)

There is always something new, and terrible, and terribly exciting captivating the conspiratorial imagination—a single conspiracy rarely satisfies a conspiracist's craving for high drama. Indeed, we Jews and Muslims have more in common than most people realize: Islamophobes invoke the same tried and untrue conspiracist narrative used to provoke fear and hatred of Jews. Déjà vu—it's uncanny indeed. Islamophobes somehow discovered the perfidious Jews' doppelganger—the Muslim Brotherhood's "Project."[16] (Some call it, "The Protocols of the Elders of Mecca."[17]) We argue that paranoia about the Brotherhood originated in the uncanny aftermath of 9/11—a humiliating assault on the American sense of self-righteousness and invulnerability. 9/11 breached the nation's defenses *and* the populations' defense mechanisms: The breach released childhood fears—the Arab became the boogeyman. We hasten to add that, unlike the Elders, the Brothers are real—*in faraway places with strange-sounding names.* Nevertheless, conspiracists imagine the Brotherhood as an imminent threat scheming on American soil. In the world according to the Islamophobe, the Brotherhood is a unitary, foreign organization with uncanny powers: Like an alien organism depicted in Marvel comics, it spreads its tentacles throughout the American body politic.

Our account deflates such histrionics.[18] Simpleminded conspiracists imagine a single, seamless brotherhood bent on subjugating, if not destroying, the West. The Brotherhoods are diverse, and no more influential in determining the course of events than your local Elks' Lodge. Even so, conspiracists such as Frank Gaffney, Jr. insist that a singular Brotherhood controls Muslim hearts and minds in America. Worse yet, the Brothers plant closet Muslims in the halls of power—"Manchurian candidates."[19] It's more ominous than you think, unless you're one of the cognoscenti who has peered behind the curtain, uncovered forbidden texts, and overheard secrets. Paranoid conspiracism attributes magic to the Brotherhoods. Fortunately, responding to this clear and present danger, the State of Oklahoma successfully prohibits the advent of Sharia law. In any event, Gaffney's 2008 jeremiads have not come to pass. Is this due to his vigilance, or could it be that his worries were unfounded?

Conspiracists traffic in a familiar fable—only the characters change. Comparisons between the Cold War Red Scare and the War on Terror Green (Muslim) Scare stand out in stark relief. No one doubts that Communist parties existed in the Soviet Union, but their influence in America varied between negligible and nonexistent—except in the conspiracist imagination. (As pundits quipped, American parties were largely composed of FBI informants.) It is worth noting that, not long ago, Mr. Gaffney promoted the Red Scare; today it's the Green Scare—more pernicious in his telling.

Islamophobes imagine that a unitary Brotherhood promotes terrorism while secretly plotting a "slow jihad" by infiltrating American culture. As Gaffney, a luminary in the conspiracist firmament, warns: "We're witnessing not just the violent kind of jihad. ... They [the Muslim Brothers] must for tactical reasons, [plot] a more stealthy kind, a civilizational jihad."[20] And don't be fooled by what Islamophobes call "pre-violent Muslims." Even seemingly moderate Muslims long for a caliphate—tyranny that would be over the top even for the dictator with the bad haircut from North Korea.

Chapter 4: Living the Dream

What possessed seemingly ordinary men such as John Earnest,[21] Robert Bowers,[22] and Brenton Tarrant[23] to murder worshipers in synagogues and mosques? We're not certain—certainty is for conspiracists, but we may have a piece of the puzzle. They were not proverbial "lone wolves." They were socialized by social media sites such as 8Chan—members of a virtual brotherhood. Their postings and manifestos reveal two fixations: anticipatory anxiety regarding changing demographics (the putative extinction of white Europeans) *and* recognition hunger—impressing their virtual brothers, if not the public at large. It is difficult to determine which fixation took priority (the shooters themselves might not know). However, we cannot rule out the possibility that the shooters' immediate craving for the bros' adulation and for notorious celebrity trumped their remote, professed hatred to those only known as imaginative abstractions. True, the shooters posted as if they were infected by Jew hatred and Islamophobia. However, much remains problematic: Do we take them at their word, or were their posts the price of admission and acclaim? However, their deeds revealed the obvious: the narcissistic enticement of celebrity culture. Craving their anon bros' (anonymous brother) adulation, the shooters boasted of their plans on their websites. Publicizing their performative violence, the shooters wanted to make a name for themselves. Tarrant—perhaps the most narcissistic among the deranged—livestreamed his cowardly crusade against the "infidels." The shooters' dream came true: They live on imprisoned in infamy.

Notes

1 Former-President Trump dismissed concern about climate change as a conspiratorial hoax. He was captivated by more exciting conspiracies involving fraudulent elections—nonexistent conspiracies evoke more passion than routine, actual collusion.

2 Colin Flint, *Spaces of Hate: Geographies of Discrimination and Intolerance in the U.S.A.* (London: Routledge, 2004), 53.

3 Interviewed by Grahme Wood, "His Kampf: Richard Spence is a Troll and an Icon for White Supremacists. He was Also my High-School Classmate." *The Atlantic*, June 6, 2017, accessed March 28, 2021, https://www.theatlantic.com/magazine/archive/2017/06/his-kampf/524505/. As we'll see, supremacists seem obsessed by their aversion to filth: Grist for the psychoanalytic mill?

4 In Chapter 4 we'll try to make sense of why this product of a seemingly ideal family, an honors student who loved Chopin, hated Jews and Muslims, endorsed conspiracies, and committed arson and murder.

5 "White Supremacist Richard Spencer Makes Racist Slurs on Tapes Released by Rival," *The Guardian,* November 4, 2019, accessed April 22, 2021, https://www.theguardian.com/world/2019/nov/04/white-supremacist-richard-spencer-racist-slurs-tape-milo-yiannopoulos.

6 Chris Cillizza, "How the Ugly, Racist White 'Replacement Theory' Came to Congress," *CNN Politics*, April 15, 2021, accessed April 17, 2021, http://www.cnn.com/2021/04/15/politics-perry-white-supremacy-theory-tucker-carlson-fox-news/index.html.

7 "Surprise: Ashkenazi Jews Are Genetically European," accessed March 29, 2021, www.livescience.com> 40247-ahkwnazi-jews-have-eur…

8 Yad Vashem, "Jewish Girl was 'Baby Poster' in Nazi Propaganda,", accessed April 22, 2021, https://www.yadvashem.org/blog/jewish-girl-was-poster-baby-in-nazi-opaganda.html.

9 Stephen Marche, *The Next Civil War: Dispatches from the American Future* (New York: Avid Reader Press / Simon & Schuster. Kindle Edition, 2022), 1.

10 Mike Rothschild, *The Storm Is Upon Us* (Brooklyn: Melville House, 2021), Kindle ed., 141. The author hastens to add that he is not related to the banking family—a perennial target of conspiracists.

11 Ava Kofman, Moira Weigel, and Francis Tseng, "White Supremacy's Gateway To The American Mind," *The Atlantic*, April 7, 2020, accessed, October 11, 2021, https://www.theatlantic.com/technology/archive/2020/04/white-supremacys-gateway-to-the-american-mind/609595/

12 Neil Postman, *Amusing Ourselves to Death: Public Discourse in the Age of Show Business* (New York: Penguin, 1985).

13 See Andrew Marantz *Anti-Social Media: Online Extremism, Techno-Utopians, and the Hijacking of the American Conversation* (New York: Viking 2019). Our account of the role of the Internet in fomenting violent conspiracism is indebted to this *New Yorker* columnist's investigations. Most telling: He interviewed white supremacist celebrity Mike Enoch who advocated gassing kikes and turning them into lampshades. Never mind his Jewish wife: His transgressive hatred bestowed Internet fame and fortune.

14 We were tempted to eschew the term "antisemitism" due to its inglorious origins in the imagination of Wilhelm Marr, a notorious 19th-century racist and Jew hater, and the fact that not all Jews are Semites; indeed, Arabs are considered Semites. However, recognizing the popular meaning of the term—and to avoid being "anti-semantic"—we'll defer to the popular meaning.

15 *The Protocols of The Learned Elders of Zion*, trans. Victor E. Marsden (Austin: RiverCrest Publishing, 2011). [Hereafter *The Protocols*.]

16 Conspiracists quest simple, uncomplicated explanations. Accordingly, they erroneously presuppose the existence of a singular, unified Brotherhood. As we'll see, a variety of organizations spanning a wide spectrum of ideology refer to themselves as the Muslim Brotherhood. Accordingly, we use the plural— "*Muslim Brotherhoods*"—when invoking our perspective.

17 See, for example, Erik Eriksen, "The Protocols of the Elders of Mecca," *Interstate—Journal of International Affairs* 2011/2012, no. 2 (2012), pp. 1–2. Just as the *Protocols* were supposedly "stumbled upon" in Switzerland, we are told that "The Project" was also stumbled upon amid a raid on a Swiss terrorist cell.

18 Asfari, a native of the Greater Middle East, reads salient documents in Arabic.

19 Actor Damian Lewis played such a role in *Homeland*, a popular TV series—a favorite of President Obama. According to the *New York Times* the president confided in Lewis: "While Michelle and the two girls go play tennis on Saturday afternoon, I go in the Oval Office, pretend I'm going to work, and then switch on *Homeland*" (August 16, 2012). Also see Hirschbein, "The Morbid Gaze: Terrorism as Entertainment," *Tikkun* 3 #1 (Winter 2016), pp. 44–48.

20 Accessed May 23, 2019, http//www.splcenter.org/fightinghate/extremicist-files/ individual/frank-gaffney-jr.

21 John T. Earnest Manifesto, accessed December 15, 2021, *edailybuzz.com/2019 /04/28/*john-earnest-manifesto.

22 See Robert Bowers' Manifesto, "Analyzing a Terrorist's Social Media Manifesto …," accessed August 20, 2019, https://www.splcenter.org/hatewatch/2018/10 /28/analyzing-terrorists-social-media-manifesto-pittsburgh-synagogue-shooters -posts-gab. Rev. Mark Schollaert, a minister who knew Bowers, describes him as: "normal . . there was never any unkindness or negativity." Accessed November 11, 2019, https://www.washingtonpost.com/national/pittsburgh -shooting-suspect-left-fleeting-impression-in-neighborhoods-he-lived-in-for -decades/2018/10/31/90e1250c-dd44-11e8-b732-3c72cbf131f2_story.html.

23 Tarrant's Manifesto, "The Great Replacement." He describes himself as "Just an ordinary White man," accessed November 8, 2019, https://www.bing.com /videos/search?q=tarrant+manifesto%2c+the+great+replacement&&view =detail&mid=8FF4.

1 Conspiracism—Modern and Postmodern

Conspiracy theory is not new, of course, but conspiracism today introduces something new—conspiracy without the theory.

Russell Muirhead and Nancy Rosenblum[1]

What is the nature of the conspiracism that stigmatizes and endangers Jews and Muslims? Prior to narrating the development of the old and the new conspiracist genres, conceptual clarity is essential—definitions are in order. Typical studies employ a fixed, dictionary definition—one size fits all. We do not. To be sure, the venerable *Oxford Dictionary* is helpful in initiating inquiry: "The belief that major historical and political events are brought about as the result of a conspiracy between interested parties or are manipulated on behalf of an unknown group of influential people." And those who embrace such conspiratorial beliefs claim that "some covert but influential agency (typically political in motivation and oppressive in intent) is responsible for an unexplained event."[2] A good start, but not the final word, for conspiracism is an evolving concept, not a thing with a fixed definition like a right triangle—it has a history.

As we've suggested, concepts with a history cannot be defined—they must be narrated, understood in context—for context determines meaning. "Conspiracism" is such a metamorphosing concept. Accordingly, we historicize the conspiratorial imagination, a sorely needed task. Most studies overlook these transformative changes. We're indebted to an exception: Muirhead and Rosenblum advance the task by contrasting two conspiracist genres: "*Classical conspiracy theory*" promulgates a grandiose narrative about how the world works and the "*new conspiracism*"[3] which eschews such ambitious grandiosity: it "dispenses with the burden of explanation"[4]— virility trumps veracity. Reframing their account, we represent conspiracism

DOI: 10.4324/9781003207894-1

on a historical continuum between the tattered texts of modernity and the pixilated postmodern.

These respective genres share a common denominator—recognition hunger. Conspiracists of every ilk seldom post, publish, or perish anonymously—they strive to make a name for themselves.[5] Of course, these respective genres satiate their recognition hunger in markedly different ways. Classical conspiracy theorists are closet theologians: They crave acclaim from awestruck readers—for *they* know a terrible truth. These self-anointed gnostics have uncovered the hidden malevolence that controls events. Like characters in a Dan Brown novel, they discover clues, connect the dots, and an ominous picture emerges: The terrible has already happened—jeremiads warn *be afraid, be terribly afraid.* Even so, they foresee a cleansing apocalypse wiping away evil and ushering in a glorious new day.

Postmodern conspiracists scoff at such ruminations. They thrive in the here and now of celebrity culture. Grand theories and millenarian visions seem ridiculous in their nihilistic world. Risible memes, not awesome revelations, bestow recognition. These latter-day conspiracists just "wanna" have fun—at another's expense.

However, before moving in for a closer look at the signature features of each genre, a caveat is in order: Modern and postmodern conspiracism are not discrete genres—there's dialectical interplay. The postmodernist' transgressive memes, vile in-jokes, and ugly slanders did not originate ex nihilo: They are derived from classics such as *The Protocols of the Learned Elders of Zion*, and the forgery's neoclassic afterlife (discussed in Chapter 2). More significant, as we'll see, Brenton Tarrant (convicted of massacring scores of New Zealand Muslims) saw postmodern amusement (the new conspiracism) strategically as a recruiting tool: a captivating enticement to entry-level conspiracism; the gateway to deadly serious classical exhortations—exterminate or be exterminated!

Classical Conspiracy Theory: A Term for all Seasons

Despite its antique vintage and promiscuous applications, the notion of "conspiracy theory" still merits attention; it has its uses. As Faulkner quipped: "The past is never dead. It's not even past." We recognize that conspiracy theory has been weaponized, and yet—on occasion—vindicated. We are, however, preoccupied with a neglected project: Analyzing its essence and inner logic. We do so by contrasting so-called conspiracy theory with actual, scientific theory: The comparison reveals conspiracy theory as perverse theology—a Manichean morality play. Finally, we turn to transgressive, postmodern conspiracism: bereft of theory, sustained argument, let alone of compelling evidence—it instantiates the new anti-intellectualism that celebrates "cognitive insolence."

Weaponizing "Conspiracy Theory"

The notion of "conspiracy theory" is weaponized and overused in mocking opponents—a weapon of choice in a polemicist's rhetorical arsenal. Its pejorative use conjures images of crackpots adorned in tin hats mumbling in their private fantasy worlds. Chomsky is a target of choice. In an otherwise measured, scholarly anthology published by Oxford University Press, sociologist Ted Goertzel argues that Chomsky should be derided as a conspiracy theorist because he claims that American political and corporate elites meet in private and, on occasion, orchestrate policies inimical to the well-being of the American public and those in other lands. (Somehow, President Eisenhower escapes the indictment despite his warnings about the machinations of the "Military-Industrial Complex" operating behind closed doors.) Like other critics, rather than disputing the arguments and evidence adduced, he dismisses Chomsky's institutional analysis of private, elite decision-making because "He does not submit his work on foreign policy to judgment by his professional peers in this way. He publishes popular books and articles in opinion journals aimed at the general public."[6] That he publishes popular books does not necessarily disprove Chomsky's evidence nor invalidate his arguments. (Indeed, the anthology in which Goertzel published is deservedly popular and referenced in popular media.)

Never mind that Chomsky explains that he is not a conspiracy theorist. He documents what hides in plain sight: how certain institutions work—institutional analysis not conspiracy theory:

> There's nothing more remote from what we have been discussing than a conspiracy theory. If … I point out that GM tries to maximize profit and market share—that's not a conspiracy theory; that's an institutional analysis. It has nothing to do with conspiracies.[7]

Indeed, there is a telling contrast between institutional analysis and *actual* conspiracism. That Ford executives strategized to maximize profit and market share was not a closely guarded conspiratorial secret—just business as usual. However, they also *conspired* in secret to conceal the inherent danger of the Ford Pinto gas tank—lives were lost.[8] It's surprising that a sociologist such as Goertzel fails to recognize elite decision-making conducted in private is business as usual, not nefarious conspiracism. As another sociologist, C. Wright Mills, quipped: Americans know they live in a time of great decisions—they know they are not making any.

Finally, weaponizing "conspiracy theory" reached a new low when Goertzel likened Bernie Sanders (a Jew whose ancestors suffered amid the Holocaust) to Nazi propagandists:

> Bernie Sanders ... used the word "rigged" frequently in his speeches.... [T]he "one percent"—rigged the entire political and economic systems. Sanders' main conspiracy theory often contradicted itself. He claimed that the wealthy had on the one hand "rigged" the economy, but on the other hand were "gambling" in the market. [Why not "gamble" in a market rigged in your favor?].... *This is the same style of rhetoric Nazi's used against the Jews—their propaganda attacked Jews for being greedy capitalists and communists.*
>
> [Ital. ours][9]

Evidence-Based Conspiracism

President Bill Clinton issued a 1997 apology, stating, "The United States government did something that was wrong—deeply, profoundly, morally wrong. In remembering that shameful past that we can make amends and repair our nation past ... [and] build a better present and a better future."[10]

Those of us who reflexively ridicule conspiracism may overlook actual conspiracism in high places. (To paraphrase the poet Bertolt Brecht—those who last laugh haven't heard the terrible news.) We're chastened when we realize that certain so-called "conspiracy theorists" sometimes get it right. Their aims are strictly limited; they are not theorists as we understand the term—they eschew grandiose narratives about how the world works. These well-tempered investigators simply seek evidence for their hypotheses. They are, in effect, *hypothetical conspiracists*. As the Tuskegee travesty illustrates—their hypotheses are sometimes vindicated. In an article aptly entitled "False Conspiracy Theory Turned Out to Be True," we learn of a young physician, Irwin Schatz, preemptively dismissed as a "conspiracy theorist." In 1965 he claimed that, in a clandestine operation beginning in 1932, the Centers for Disease Control deceived 399 African American men about their syphilis infections; they were told blood samples were drawn to treat "bad blood." These subjects were not treated with effective antibiotics when they became available. (Apparently, at autopsy, investigators wanted to determine the pathology caused by this untreated disease.) Eventually, further publicity led to investigations that prompted President Clinton's apology.[11]

Turning to a more recent instance, it seems Chomsky can't win: He is also chastised for indicting an *actual* conspiracy in high places. He claimed that the Bush Administration manufactured consent for an invasion of Iraq by promoting anxiety about fictitious weapons of mass destruction (WMDs).[12] Critics derided his claim as "conspiracy theory." The "Downing Street Memos" vindicated his allegations: Evidently, President Bush and Prime Minister Tony Blair conspired to invade Iraq and to depose Hussein—they had their reasons.[13] WMDs were a very good reason for war; the real reasons involved geopolitics and oil. No weapons were found: "Shock and Awe" became "Aw shucks!" As philosopher Charles Pigden argues, falsely charging "conspiracy theory" camouflages *actual* conspiracism:

> That conspiracy theories are suspect was used ... to deflect attention from [Blair's]conspiracy, thus helping to justify a war which resulted in hundreds of thousands of unnecessary deaths. Conspiracy theories can kill but so can the idea that they are ... always false.[14]

To be sure, conspiracy theories can kill—or sanction killing—be they true or false. However, "conspiracy theory" per se is a misnomer. The essence of so-called conspiracy becomes evident when compared to actual, scientific theory. In our telling, so-called theories are perverse, Manichean theologies.

Scientific Theory v. Conspiracy Theory

> Conspiracy theories are the way they are because they're a product of someone's imagination, and they're popular because they align with other peoples' imaginations. What kind of people tend to think this way, and why? That requires a little more explaining.
>
> Rob Brotherton[15]

We do "a little more explaining." Scientific theory is about empirical reality; conspiracy theory is imaginative. We recognize that some explaining is done through the usual social-scientific approaches: interviews, surveys, and questionnaire responses.[16] However, these explanations overlook the theological dimensions that simultaneously inspire and twist the supremacist's conspiratorial imagination.

Accordingly, we do more explaining by turning to the humanities and invoking what interpretive anthropologist Clifford Geertz called "thick descriptions"—explanations attentive to historical context and to lived experience. As anthropologist Katherine Hoffman explains: "The use of metaphor and imagery was central to Geertz's vision of a revamped social science, and especially anthropology, that would take its cues as much from the humanities as the hard sciences."[17] Metaphors (to speak metaphorically) are a key to unlocking a subject's imaginative world. The arresting metaphors of so-called conspiracy theory reveal the assumptions that inform the white supremacists' imaginative, conspiratorial accounts of Jews and Muslims.

Scientists and conspiracists do have something in common. They devise imaginative metaphors. Of course, their origins and entailments are radically different. *Scientific theorizing begins with novel metaphors and ends in mathematically precise, often accurate, predictions. Conspiracy theorizing begins with time-dishonored metaphors and survives regardless of false predictions.*

Scientific metaphors often begin in a flash of original insight—a novel connection between unlike domains. Hackneyed, conspiracist metaphors—that demean Jews and Muslims—are transmitted through a long-established zeitgeist sanctioned by hoary authority. The scientific imagination generates original metaphors that promotes rigorous observation and experimentation: inquiry leading to explanations of how the world works. Unlike conspiracy theory, scientific theory facilitates the prediction and control of nature.

The changeless metaphors that inform conspiracism arrest inquiry; unlike science at its best, conspiracism is close-minded. Conspiracists are convinced they're attained what philosopher Richard Rorty called a "final vocabulary"—in this case the last word on Jews and Muslims, an irrefutable credo. Conspiracy theorists cling to their cherished metaphors with religious zeal. What inquiry occurs is driven by confirmation bias, cognitive dissonance is ignored, and metaphors are not seen for what they are—tendentious, imaginative constructions. By way of contrast, the history of science chronicles the advent of fresh, novel metaphors. Newton envisioned the world as a machine, a metaphor once appropriated by mechanistic approaches to genetics and much else. Amid the computer age, geneticists liken the human genome to a program—DNA is akin to a computer code.

Newton's metaphorical flash is the stuff of legend. In 1665, amid the plague, he left Cambridge University and returned to the family estate. There—or so the oft' told tale goes—he observed fruit falling to earth in the orchard. He likened the falling fruit to the moon "falling" to earth—a resonant metaphor that sparked the notion of gravity in young Isaac's imagination. His signature project began. Like his predecessors he was perplexed by a mystery—"action at a distance" was baffling and it still is. Einstein called it "spooky action" for good reason: Objects affect one another without physical contact.[18] Proceeding inductively, Newton observed, experimented, and synthesized the discoveries and insights of his predecessors. Generalizing from a coherent set of data, he formulated laws of motion still applicable beyond the subatomic realm. (Even now his laws plot the trajectories of spacecraft and much else.)

Newton attained everlasting fame for discovering and formulating a particle logic—the gravitational essence of matter: You'll recall from high school physics that any two masses attract each other—a universal attraction immutable in the South of France or on South Neptune: Every particle attracts every other particle in the universe with a force directly proportional to the product of its masses and inversely proportional to the square of the distance between their centers. Formulated mathematically, the law—to understate the case—has been tested and subjected to possible falsification—the hallmark of legitimate science. Poet Alexander Pope rhapsodized about Newtonian enlightenment: "Nature, and Nature's Laws lay hid in Night, God said, 'Let Newton be!' and All was Light."

The Jew never lay hid in night—not in the conspiracist imagination. Classical conspiracy theory shines an eerie light on universal, eternal Jewish malevolence. Just as particles repulse one another in Newtonian particle logic, conspiracists are repulsed by Jews and Muslims be they from the South of France or from South Neptune. Newton sought natural causes for events; supremacist conspiracists prefer to look for Jews and Muslims. Speaking of plagues, as Alyssa Weiner explains:

> For centuries antisemites have blamed Jews for global pandemics, so it is no surprise that conspiracy theories are circulating linking Jews and Israel with the novel coronavirus COVID-19. They combine several common antisemitic tropes, including dirty Jews spreading infection and Jews getting rich by exploiting a defenseless public.[19]

Conspiracists base their phobia and hatred of Jews and Muslims upon universal generalizations akin to absolute, immutable Newtonian laws. Unlike testable scientific laws, conspiracist "laws" are not derived inductively through sustained, systematic research and testing. They are *deductive*, true by definition—immune to falsification. No research agenda is prescribed. As Georgetown Law Professor David Luban observes:

> Conspiracy theories ... partake of supersense – and, as [Hannah] Arendt notes, they also resemble the mental constructions of paranoiacs, where everything follows inexorably from a delusional first premise; ... the insanity lies not only in the premise but also in the sheer logicality by which every observable fact snaps crisply into place within the theory.[20]

Just as the fabled scientist discovered the universal, inexorable laws of nature, conspiracists are confident that they too have discovered universal laws governing Jewish and Muslim sensibility and behavior. John Earnest (convicted of arson and murder in suburban San Diego) shared his "discovery" in his Manifesto—a universal law governing Jewish behavior. "Every Jew is responsible for the meticulously planned genocide of the European race. They act as a unit, and every Jew plays his part to enslave the other races around him—whether consciously or subconsciously."[21] Earnest doesn't present evidence for his breathtaking generalization; no need, it's self-evident to Earnest and to other Jew haters. The generalization, of course, is not original; it reflects a long and sordid history of paranoid bigotry.

Internet sites have de facto gatekeeping requirements—a price of admission. Demonizing Jews and Muslims is requisite for acceptance and acclaim. Earnest, in effect, pledged a brotherhood. His need for fraternal approval spun this honors student's moral compass. Luban reiterates Hannah Arendt's insight:

> The goal of propaganda is not persuasion but organization ... Organization aims at recruiting [initiates] to a tribe ... The only truth that matters is ... tribal identity. What matters isn't factual reality, but the reality of "us," the real people, in contrast to the poisonous subtlety of "them," the tribal adversary.[22]

Unlike scientists, conspiracy theorists ignore cognitive dissonance. Earnest was no exception. This member in good standing of a nearby Orthodox Presbyterian church expressed his devotion to Christianity. But somehow the law of Jewish malevolence did not apply to Jesus—the Jewish carpenter Earnest claims to worship. Dissonance and other cognitive concerns matter to academics, not to conspiracists.

Like most products in the culture of the spectator and commodity, conspiracy theories have expiration dates—truth matters not at all: A theory flourishes if it's novel, shocking, and absurd but vanishes if it becomes timeworn and boring—a loser in competition with the newfound sensational, and lurid. (The JFK assassination and Birther theories—your daddy's conspiracies—are no match for QAnon revelations of satanic pedophiles in high places.) Like any addict, conspiracy theorists seek a more energizing fix—classic Judeophobia isn't enough.

Fantasies about Muslim treachery once lay hid in night—at least in American popular culture. No more. 9/11 revealed a startling, uncanny truth to conspiracists longing for fresh enemies—the Muslim's are coming! In her *Eurabia*, Bat Ye'or somehow discovered *the* inexorable, universal law of Muslim treachery. Just as Newtonian law applies to all matter, she grasps the essence of *all* Muslims, be they Syrian Arabs, Polynesian Indonesians, or decidedly unexotic American CPAs: "The entire Muslim world as we know it today is a product of this 1,300 year old *jihad* dynamic."[23]

Islamophobes vow that Vienna will not be Istanbul. The Sultan's legions are not at the gates of Vienna again—not yet. Cunning Muslims conquer through "slow jihad." Nations are being destroyed from without and from within by jihadist terrorist cells metastasizing throughout the body politic. Such Islamophobia is hardly novel; Muslims were long demonized and dreaded in European thought. However, in American popular culture, for the most part, Islamophobia is a post-9/11 development. As we'll see, prior to that fateful day, the Muslim (again, conflated with the Arab) was reduced to a benign Orientalism—the magical Arab of Disney cartoons. The aftermath of 9/11 transformed the Muslim from genie to boogeyman. Seen through a Freudian lens, 9/11 was uncanny. It released long-repressed anxieties that bedevil children in their febrile dreams.

The *Protocols*' doppelganger, "The Project," depicts this demonized group as a formidable conspiracy bent upon planetary tyranny. In the aftermath of 9/11 anyone who appeared Middle Eastern evoked puerile panic. (An Italian professor of mathematics was removed from a commercial aircraft due to his suspicious Mediterranean appearance and mysterious calculations—no doubt reckoned in Arabic numerals.[24])

Given their confirmation bias, conspiracy theorists never meet a derogatory anecdote, trope, or fiction about Jews and Muslims they don't like. Seemingly trivial, unrelated events have hidden meanings; connecting the dots uncovers a terrible truth. The denouement of the white supremacist narrative is preordained—no suspense as we read the *Protocols* or the "Project" The clues invariably lead to the preordained conclusion—Jews and Muslims ceaselessly scheme to commit white genocide and to rule the world. Don't ask for proof—it's page-turning fiction.

The Truth About the Falsification Principle

> In so far as a scientific statement speaks about reality, it must be falsifiable, and in so far as it is not falsifiable, it does not speak about reality.
>
> Karl Popper[25]

The truth is that conspiracy theorists could care less about Karl Popper. Audacious recognition trumps respectable, falsifiable evidence. True to our professions, we cherish the principle—a telling contrast between science and conspiracy theory. Indeed, those of us in the social sciences and humanities suffer physics-envy: We're in awe of the highly acclaimed, falsifiable predictions that emerge from our colleagues in other buildings. Humbled, and at our best, we meekly acknowledge the unhappy limitations of our "human sciences." Conspiracy theorists are seldom accused of humility.

These so-called theorists don't share our concerns—they're immune to evidence and to embarrassment. We effortlessly discover their failed predictions; we've yet to discover conspiracists apologizing for the error of their ways. It's nothing new: In promoting the *Protocols* in 1903, the Russian mystic, Sergei Nilus prophesied the imminent arrival of the Antichrist and unspeakable Jewish tyranny. However, inspired perhaps by the *Protocols*, tyranny *did* arrive—for the Jews who perished in Cossack pogroms. Litigation and scholarship proving that the *Protocols* was a forgery didn't stop Henry Ford from distributing 500,000 copies and promoting the document and its calumnies in his Dearborn, Michigan paper.

Moving forward to au courant conspiracism, QAnon breaks with tradition by hazarding readily falsifiable precise predictions: Contrary to these continually revised forecasts, former-President Trump was not reinstated on: January 20, 2021, March 4, 2021, or August 13, 2021—an unlucky Friday the 13th for true believers. The anointed days passed with a whimper, not a bang. Even so, standing before the gates of the deep state hell, the faithful do not abandon all hope. Writing in *Forbes* Nicholas Reimann suggests the faithful still await Trump's second coming.[26]

Such readily falsified predictions rarely trouble conspiracists who usually respond with profound indifference or redoubled devotion. On rare occasions they default to a predictable ploy. As philosopher Brian Keely notes, conspiracists prevaricate to disguise falsified predictions. Unlike scientists, conspiracists introduce convenient game-changers: Duplicitous human (or supernatural) agency moves the proverbial goalposts with the game in play. Lest their breathtaking claims be falsified, conspiracists rationalize that:

> Powerful, conniving agents safeguard secrets … disguise their malevolent intentions. [Unlike the objects of scientific inquiry] the *subjects* of investigation "actively seek to hamper the investigation. Imagine if neutrinos were not simply hard to detect, but actively sought to avoid detection!"[27]

The rare theorist, troubled by failed prophesy, may resort to bizarre rationalizations—claims more absurd than the theories themselves. Does Trump still rule disguised as Biden? Responding to this QAnon posting, reporter, Bill McEwen asks: "Have you heard the one about Biden's Face on Trump's body?"[28] It does no good to indict such absurdities: They're the main attraction.

Are conspiracists flattered by us epistemological vigilantes—do they relish our attention? Or perhaps we protest too much? Do they suspect that, at some subliminal level, even unenlightened academics know that something ain't right. Our preoccupation with falsification reaffirms what the conspiracist already knew: Bereft of the conspiracist's incite and courage, we academics cannot abide the unthinkable. Despite—or because of—our credentials, we are akin to the other naïve "sheeple" led to the slaughter by other pseudo-intellectuals attuned to fake news. Worse yet, maybe we skeptics are in league with the conspiracists themselves?

We share analyst Rob Brotherton's "futilitarianism" regarding debating conspiracists: "You can't win when you're fighting a conspiracy that doesn't exist."[29] As he concludes:

> Conspiracy theories aren't just immune to refutation — they thrive on it. If it looks like a conspiracy, it was a conspiracy. If it doesn't look like a conspiracy, it was definitely a conspiracy. Evidence against the conspiracy theory becomes evidence of conspiracy. Heads I win, tails you lose.[30]

What conclusion should be drawn from the inner illogic of conspiracy theorizing? Given his epistemological vigilance, political scientist Joe Uscinski concludes: "If there is no evidence that would falsify a conspiracy theory … then it is no longer theory; it is theology."[31] Uscinski doesn't probe the theology. We do.

Conspiracy Theory as Theology

Epistemological vigilantes don't get it if they preemptively dismiss conspiracy theory because it can't be falsified. True, such theorizing cannot be justified in our terms, *but can it be understood? Preoccupied with reasoning, epistemological vigilantes miss the theological meaning.* Writing in *Episteme*, philosopher Glen Bezalel reminds us that a worldview that cannot be falsified can be redolent with meaning.[32] Such a worldview—a hermetically sealed bundle of cherished beliefs, values, and spirations—infuses life with meaning, direction, and purpose. Immune to criticism, let alone falsification, cherished, invincible doctrines enjoy power and permanence—for good or evil. The great religions—faiths that call forth our better angels *and* our worse demons—cannot be falsified, at least this side of eternity.

Sacrosanct conspiracy theories—a rock of ages in a vertiginous world—are not mere myths; they are much more—an unshakable, albeit perverse, theology. Myths, as we understand them, are traditional, widely held fables regarding an event or person. Their authorship is generally unknown or irrelevant. Not so in theology: Authorship bestows credibility and fame—or misfortune—upon the author. (Would Thomas Aquinas be a saint if his *Summa* were published anonymously?) Who knows how myths originate? As children we learned that George Washington could not tell a lie—he confessed to chopping down the cherry tree. These days we read childish myths that pander to inveterate narcissism: Bill Gates infuses COVID vaccines with nanochips to monitor our behavior. (Apparently, the Seattle billionaire has nothing better to do than to track our activity.)

Conspiracist theology is an all-encompassing metanarrative: a timeless account of an incredibly powerful, malevolent agency overseeing the past, present, and future. This synoptic perspective addresses a matter of ultimate concern—the very fate of humanity. In this seamless worldview (at once, congenial and disturbing) there are no accidents, no random events—all is planned. Things are not what they seem in a matrix of hidden meanings. Given the agent's master plan, there are no discrete events—everything is somehow connected. No wonder, writing in *Personality and Social Psychology*, Franks and Bangerter conclude: "Our key claim is that CTs [conspiracy theories] have contents and functions that are quasi-religious: there is an analogy between religious beliefs and ... the ways in which CT typically construe ... conspirators."[33]

As the authors caution, they are merely drawing an analogy between conspiracy theory and religion. (Analogies tendentiously highlight similarities between domains while underplaying differences.) The authors realize that Presbyterian congregants and QAnon true believers are not the same. That said, the perverse assumptions of conspiracy theory become blatantly transparent when deconstructed into theological categories.

The theological foundation of conspiracism—redolent with passion and purpose—stands out in bold relief in a disenchanted world bereft of tradition and meaning. Questioning white privilege is under assault: Supremacists embrace their special dispensation with religious fervor. Supremacist theology is what philosopher Raymond Aron might call a secular religion. As we'll see in analyzing the *Protocols* and its neoclassic legacy, such a faith is anthropocentric, not theocentric. Like traditional religion it looks forward to redemption and salvation; however, no deus ex machina intervenes. Only heroic human intervention can usher in a glorious future: a history written by men, not by gods. Of course, prophesying glory in some remote future is a bad career move for aspiring prophets; consumers crave immediate gratification yesterday. No wonder conspiracist canon declares that the end time nears; salvation is at hand.[34]

Such is the backdrop, the staging, for conspiracist theology. However, immediate, more prosaic circumstances foment an energizing dogma that temporarily satiates recognition of hunger, and perhaps more significant, assuages a chronic malady of life in these United States—boredom.

Bored to Fears

To reiterate, we recognize that conspiracy theologies are imaginative attempts to render the unintelligible intelligible: to make sense of what psychologist William James called a world of blooming, buzzing confusion. But man doesn't live by cognition alone. That conspiracism may salve gnawing boredom is rarely considered. As we'll see in recounting the saga of Sergei Nilus—the first promoter of the *Protocols*—conspiracism can begin in boredom and climax in fanaticism.

Psychologists Brotherton and Esers introduce boredom as a factor in understanding conspiracism. It's as if they had Our Candidate in mind when they authored "Bored to Fears: Boredom Proneness, Paranoia, and Conspiracy Theories." They found a telling correlation between the schizotypical disorder and conspiracism: "The proclivity to become bored easily—is a stable personality trait which has been reported to be associated with this disorder."[35] The Mayo Clinic describes individuals suffering this disorder in more detail as:

> Odd or eccentric [those who suffer this disorder] usually have few, if any, close relationships. They may also misinterpret others' motivations and behaviors and develop significant distrust of others. These problems may lead to severe anxiety and a tendency to avoid social situations, as the person with schizotypal personality disorder tends to hold peculiar beliefs.[36]

According to the authors the "peculiar beliefs" include paranoid ideation about a powerful, vexatious agency causing their woes. Unable to resist cliches, we imagine Our Candidate isolated in his parents' basement, entranced by a conspiracist website, in search of virtual friendship and recognition. The quest, of course, may be in vain. However, at least engrossing "theories" regarding Jewish and Muslim perfidy may amuse and relieve boredom, if only for an hour or two: Unfortunately, temporary relief provided by random reinforcement, reinforces addiction. Sharing their research in the *British Journal of Psychology*, Prooijen, Ligthart, Rosema, and Xu conclude that "One reason why people believe conspiracy theories is because they find them entertaining." (*Amusing Ourselves to Death*, Neil Postman's account of entertainment as the métier of American culture, gains newfound resonance in their study.[37])

Their conclusion is based upon five incidents featured in popular media. The studies include accounts of the death of Jeffrey Epstein, the Notre Dame fire, and a recent presidential election. Subjects were exposed to either non-conspiratorial accounts of the events—dull, matter-of-fact reportage—or classically conspiratorial accounts—intended to be "interesting, exciting, and attention-grabbing." Not surprisingly, the latter elicited rapt attention, strong affect, and a will to believe the conspiratorial narrative.[38]

We've suggested an unnerving symmetry: The deeper the boredom, the more soaring the engrossing fantasies. Recall that an interlocutor urged Our Candidate to conquer despair by making a name for himself in Amazon's self-publishing world. We do not know whether this dissipated individual took this advice. Perhaps, inspired by the exchange, he sought infamy in conjuring an "indisputable" exposé of Jewish pedophiles." However, writing a book is not always the best palliative for boredom, let alone a fount of amusement (unless anxiety is preferable to boredom.) We would not be surprised to learn that the troubled lad might have temporarily conquered boredom and attained recognition by transforming the theological dogmas that follow into iconic memes on the postmodern Internet. QAnon might prove enticing.

The Canons of White Supremacy

Worship

White supremacists derive meaning from sacralizing their fantasies—venerating themselves and their imagined racial purity. Supremacists are not the first idolators to worship themselves. Xenophanes, the ancient Greek poet, noted that people create their gods in their own image: The Thracian people had blue eyes and red hair—so did their gods. Durkheim had good reason for claiming that religion is the worship of one's group. Supremacists never tire of praising their imagined race.[39]

We've heard their devotional, 14-word credo: "We must secure the existence of our people and a future for white children." The pious utter their own bizarre "Ave Maria" recitative to the mothers of white gods: "The beauty of the White Aryan woman must not perish from the earth." Like most faiths, supremacist theology proscribes sacred times and spaces. Neo-Nazis celebrate Hitler's birthday; perhaps January 6 (the Capitol Insurrection) will become a celebrated holiday. Religious venues are of course sacred spaces. As we'll see from manuscripts posted by Bowers and Tarrant, supremacists were enraged when their sacred spaces were profaned by people of color and faux-white Jews.

And yet, the Hebrew Bible is instructive: Supremacist self-deification has a decidedly Old Testament ring. In *Exodus* we find a vindictive God, lacking a Christian attitude, admonishing the tremulous Hebrews: The LORD thy God is a jealous God ... lest the anger of the LORD thy God be kindled against thee and destroy thee from off the face of the earth. *I am the LORD your God. "You shall have no other gods before me."* White supremacists are jealous breed: Thou shalt have no other races before them: Black lives don't matter, and white genocide will punish the unforgivable sins of multiculturalism.

Revelation

Conspiracies are not discovered through personal contact, let alone through meticulous research.[40] As we've seen, older conspiracists still rely upon the prevailing zeitgeist—classical and neoclassical texts sanctify their narcissism, hatreds, and fears. As studies of the mass psychology of fascism have long revealed, rallies and marches spread the word: A number of supremacist groups recruit by scapegoating Jews and Muslims along with heart-pounding dress-up charades: Life is indeed dull without enemies and reckless adventures—marching with the Proud Boys. As we've suggested, endorsing such a theology—reverently confessing those 14 words—may be the price of admission and camaraderie. (Indeed, we cannot help but wonder: Do the supremacists who stigmatize and endanger us really hate us, or do they simply need a brief refuge from boredom in an ersatz brotherhood, or the make-believe excitement of playing soldier? Do they know themselves?)

We locate Brenton Tarrant on a liminal point on our continuum—betwixt and between modernity and postmodernism. As we'll see in Chapter 2, the neoclassic texts of modernity still cast their spell. However, Tarrant found a luminous source of ultimate enlightenment: Like the other shooters, he got his ideas about Replacement Theory shattered into memes and slurs, on 8chan: "[I] received, researched, and developed my beliefs, from the internet, of course. You will not find the truth anywhere else."[41]

Gnosticism

Conspiracy theologians commit the sin of pride. They insist that they, and only they, know terrible secrets. Should we take them at their word—do they actually believe what they say? But no question about it: They try to convince others that—unlike ordinary mortals—they possess secret knowledge of nefarious, conspiratorial schemes. What are their priorities? Wouldn't it be prudent to keep secrets, lest the clandestine evildoers know they've been discovered? The neo-gnostics audaciously boast about their forbidden knowledge. Unique, personal recognition is valued above all else.

Theodicy

Conspiracy theories ... have little or nothing to do with science. "In place of impersonal, law-governed forces ... they substitute evil cabals executing secret plots."[42] As we'll see in the *Protocols*, the demonized 19th-century Jew replaces the medieval devil. The latter-day white supremacist imagination is a cartoon world of good guys fighting bad guys—as seen on TV. The good guys wear white cowboy or MAGA hats; the bad guys crown their evil with kippahs or kufis. In this Marvel comic world, the bad guys are not evil due to unfortunate circumstances. Conspiracists have no interest in delving into the interstices of inconclusive sociological studies and contesting theories. They seem captivated by the iconic images of popular culture: Who cares about the childhood of the ugly, evil emperor in *Star Wars*? Fans crave plain and simple dramaturgy in which bad guys are intrinsically and irredeemably evil. Evildoers are never weak and inept, nor are they plagued by self-doubts and remorse—they're inhuman. (Woody Allen would not be cast as the emperor.) In addition to superhuman strength, evildoers are omniscient and omnipotent—an inevitable challenge for those who would vanquish evil.

The identity of formidable, secret evildoers varies, but Jews invariably make the list, and no list would be complete today without Muslims. A brief motley sample might also include the Illuminati, Jesuits, and the Masons.[43] These diverse cabals have something in common: Their evil motivation is thematic, not episodic. (Bat Ye'or does not tepidly warn, that now and then, like everyone else, Muslims do a few deplorable deeds; such a modest claim would make the other all-too-ordinary.) The cabals are deemed intrinsically and irredeemably evil whether due to race, captivating ideology, or satanic enchantment. (Satan, long absent in classics such as the *Protocols*, makes a cameo appearance in QAnon.) Even apart from Satan, Jews and Muslims pose an ominous threat—they must be thwarted or eliminated if they imagine white race, nature's greatest miracle, is to survive and flourish.

The ludicrous, make-believe threat bespeaks of Hofstadter's apprehension about the paranoic style of American politics. In the United States, Jews and Muslims constitute a small fraction of the population. (Pew Research estimates about 1% Muslim and 2.5% Jewish.[44]) Despite the diversity and contention within each group, conspiracists claim that Muslims and Jews act as singular units. Curiously, the conspiracist confronts the same mystery that bedevils physics—*action at a distance*. Conspiracy theorists, who pride themselves in connecting the dots, never reveal the processes and mechanics: how the cabal pulls the strings. (Like the Almighty, conspirators work in mysterious ways.) However, on occasion, when they attend to such questions, they offer vacuous assertions about the Rothschilds' money and other international bankers, somehow orchestrating world-historical events such as wars and revolutions—but there is no proof. The faithful just know what we Jews and Muslims have in store for them. Even so, in the world according to white supremacy, seemingly overwhelming evil can be vanquished if white knights awaken from their media-induced slumber and do what must be done. Faith-based conspiracists know that history can have a happy ending.

Eschatology

Eschatology conjures visions of the final days, the end of history. As Norman Cohn—noted for his influential account of the *Protocols*—explains: "The vision offers the fervent hope of this-worldly salvation—heaven on earth."[45] Of course, utopia is only for the truly deserving, the elect. Historically, evil forces have prevented the chosen from attaining what they so righteously deserve. Vanquishing evil will usher in a happy ending for the just and righteous.

This narrative, be it the apocalyptic reckoning in the *Book of Revelation* or QAnon visions of the "The Storm," emboldens individuals to vent their most fervent, sadistic longings. The conspiracy theorist literature features lurid scenarios of the last days of the sworn enemies of the white race. Echoing *The Turner Diaries*, the Earnest Manifesto anticipates "The Day of the Rope": white supremacists will hang their enemies while taking gleeful vengeance on "race traitors"—whites who betray their heritage. When the QAnon Storm is upon us, the Satan-worshiping minions of Hillary Clinton will surely be executed for killing children and imbibing their blood. The cleansing apocalypse sets the pristine scene for a paradisiacal existence.

For Nazis and neo-Nazis the cleansing means genocide. However, urbane, clean-cut Richard Spencer, put off by blood and bile, won't dirty his well-manicured hands. He envisages a thoughtfully planned, nonviolent ethnic cleansing deporting undesirables to other locations—he would kindly ask the lesser breeds to leave—in the interest of "racial realism." Spencer's litany iterates the Supremacist Credo promising salvation at the end of days. He echoes a Nazi slogan—*The future belongs to us.*[46] Posterity, in Spencer's homiletics: "Belongs to white men. Our bones are in the ground. We own it. At the end of the day America can't exist without us. We defined it. This country does belong to White people, culturally, politically, socially, everything."[47]

The Turn toward Postmodernism

Conspiracy theology is not obsolete; it has its uses. Postmodern Internet tropes, memes, and in-jokes are familiar to those who read the *Protocols*. But who reads these days? We suspect we're not the only academics who hector students about our unfair, classroom competition—cellphones. Students reflexively turn to apps configured to capture their attention. Does novelist Julia Bell exaggerate when she laments: "When we're not online … [t]he non-digital world feels increasingly strange and perhaps even boring."[48] No wonder conspiracists like Tarrant entice young men hooked on the scurrilous Internet and its macho-psychotic videogames.

We've invoked the term "postmodern" here with some abandon. Is a definition possible, let alone desirable? Is it just another trendy term to be bandied about like "surreal?" Perhaps it's like obscenity—you know it when you see it. We appreciate the irony in trying to define the term, for postmodernists mock assigning fixed meanings to concepts—especially to *their* concepts. Worse yet, postmodernists hermetically seal themselves in arcane jargon—as if to ward off the uninitiated, to say nothing of critique. In any case, concision is not their most endearing virtue. However, modest clarity can be had: Writing in *The Postmodern Condition*, Jean-François Lyotard (preeminent among postmodernists) offers an oft-quoted, succinct definition: "incredulity towards metanarratives."[49] Not only are postmodern conspiracists incredulous toward grandiose theories, they ignore and mock them.

Even so, grandiose conspiracy narratives such as the *Protocols* lead an afterlife. As we'll see, the fabrication constructs and synthesizes centuries of Jew hatred into a coherent conspiracist saga. Postmodern conspiracism inverts the process by deconstructing coherent, classical theory into transgressive shards: vile memes, crude tropes, and vulgar in-jokes—the métier of the conspiracist Internet. Postmodern conspiracism is about addictive entertainment, not somber truth. It traffics in bizarre tales and attention-grabbing assertions, not reasoned, persuasive discourse. In so doing, deconstructed conspiracy theology transforms paranoid fantasies from the printed page into captivating Internet memes and much else.

No sense wondering whether these deconstructions are true—you'd miss the point! One doesn't read fiction or indulge in postmodern reverie to discover obdurate truths. Indeed, there is considerable controversy about whether those who post on these sites mean to be taken seriously. Muirhead and Rosenbaum detect a pronounced nihilism in the new (postmodern conspiracism) conspiracism. Postings are not informed by theories, nor are they prescriptive or aspirational. Like Hofstadter before them, they witness the catharsis of angry minds seeking:

> The immediate gratification of lashing out, of throwing verbal stones … A particularly gratifying form of vilification … the more unfathomable the accusation, the greater degree of disorientation, incredulity, and rage it provokes in its targets.[50]

As the authors urge, what we dub postmodern conspiracism is politically sterile—devoid of grandiose schemes and glorious goals. It's "destabilizing, degrading, deconstructing, and delegitimizing, without a countervailing impulse."[51] Such apparent nihilism isn't wholly devoid of ideals—if narcissistic aspirations can be deemed ideals. Craving notoriety, jesters struggle to make a name for themselves as they vie to post the most cringe-worthy memes. They delight in schadenfreude—relishing another's misery. (There's considerable controversy regarding whether cringe-worthy postings should be taken seriously; indeed, those who post might not know themselves.) How much does it exaggerate to liken postmodern conspiracists to two debased cartoon characters—Beavis and Butt-head? Their episodes pivot around depraved trash-talk and misdeeds. If these delinquent teenage couch potatoes are not out causing mayhem:

> They're ... watching TV, or looking at pornographic magazines. Both lack any empathy or moral scruples ... They will usually deem their encounters as "cool" if they are associated with ... violence, sex, destruction, or the macabre ... Their actions sometimes result in serious consequences, sometimes for themselves but often for others.[52]

Unlike the theologians mentioned above, these latter-day conspiracists care not about how history works or ends—they don't prophesize about a world to come. Immersed in the here and now, they seek recognition as transgressors. In posting offensive memes they are not unlike these teenage delinquents spray-painting graffiti. Driven by insatiable recognition hunger, they gorge on cringe-worthy comments and revel in Internet charades in which wannabe heroes fancy themselves as knight crusaders or Nordic heroes. They indulge in a raucously entertaining, virtual world in which we are stigmatized by their risible memes and vile in-jokes. More disturbing: We are endangered when a postmodern conspiracist stops joking and becomes a deadly serious competitor vying for the highest kill score. Our distraught youth might find himself on the websites of the likes of Brenton Tarrant.

The Postmodern Internet

> Whilst we may use edgy humour and memes in the vanguard stage, and to attract a young audience, eventually we will need to show the reality of our thoughts and our more serious intents and wishes for the future. For now we appeal to the anger and black comedic nature of the present, but eventually we will need to show the warmth and genuine love we have for our people.
>
> Brenton Tarrant[53]

Tarrant, recruited for his race war against interlopers profaning white spaces. Like other latter-day conspiracists he knew that the fun and games of postmodern conspiracism would be more enticing than the tedious texts of conspiracy theology. For Tarrant, warmth and love meant joining him in massacring innocent Muslim worshippers.

Writing in *Kill All Normies*, Angela Nagle avoids convoluted jargon and writes clearly about the postmodern reverie that besmirches the Internet with "weird pornography … gory images … and murderous and incestuous thoughts." She says it best when she quips the conspiracist posting on the likes of 4chan and 8chan "read like the inside of a high-school bathroom stall."[54]

We are not shocked by the graffiti, but, like Nagle, we regret the Internet's betrayal of its promise. The promised joyride on the information highway has far right exits onto the autobahn of neo-Nazi traffic. The cyber-utopians thought the Internet foretold the apotheosis of democratic dialogue—all voices would be heard and respected in a cybernated New England-style town meeting. Pornography became a bigger attraction: Softcore *Playboy*-style images of the pretty nude girl next door got a few hits; perversity that would embarrass the Marquis De Sade proved irresistible: "The Anime Death Tentacle Rape Whorehouse … grew to around 750 million page views a month." The safety and anonymity of the keyboard encouraged: "the grim flowering of the id's voodoo energies." [55]

The flowering bespeaks of ghastly horrors. Addicted QAnon followers revive an ancient blood libel: Satan-worshiping Democrats kill babies and drink their blood.[56] Curiously, the followers lack appropriate affect—they aren't horrified—they seem amused. An entertaining horror show trumps boredom any time. Unlike the theologians, the Internet narcissists don't hazard knowledge claims. As Muirhead and Rosenblum explain:

> The new conspiracism—all accusation, no evidence—substitute social validation for scientific validation: if a lot of people are saying it, to use Trump's signature phrase, then it is true [or entertaining] enough.[57]

The Clintons are frequently targeted by evidence-free accusations—tendentious questions that capture attention and titillate. Gwen Farrell is just asking: "What Is Going On? 57 People From Bill And Hillary Clinton's Inner Circle Have Died In Strange Circumstances In The Last 30 Years."[58] Our Candidate might have a good time, if like a learned philosopher, he asked the right questions. However, first he would need to learn the basics of the postmodern Internet. In this medium, virality trumps veracity.

- *The Lulz*

Forget your moral compass and enjoy the lulz. This play on the tradition LOL (lots of laughs) emphasizes schadenfreude. Sacrosanct, previously untouchable topics such as the Holocaust are a favorite target of transgressive postings and public displays. An "edgelord" is lauded as a master of transgression. Nagel was prescient: "If this dark, anti-Semitic ... ideology grows in the coming years, with ... vision that would necessitate violence, those who made [this] attractive will have to take responsibility for their role."[59] A capitol insurrectionist's "Camp Auschwitz" shirt made an indelible impression.

- *The Memes*

Memes reflect this postmodern insensibility.[60] What is a meme? Everyone seems to know until he or she is asked to define it—the meaning is elusive. For now, suffice it to mention that most definitions begin with reference to Richard Dawkin's *The Selfish Gene*. Memes are likened to viruses for good reason: These contagious fragments of cultural ideas and behavior spread through a large population. Like a funhouse mirror for culture and society, they reflect and refract the anxieties and preoccupations of a variety of social groups across a series of national contexts. Those of concern in this context stigmatize Jews and Muslims. A typical cringe-worthy meme mocks the Holocaust or portrays the Arab as a savage terrorist. Chapter 4 moves in for a closer look at the nature and role of memes in promoting conspiracism.

T.S. Elliot was prescient when he wrote *The Hollow Men* nearly one hundred years ago. He wrote amid decay and passionless decadence. We wonder whether the authors had the poet in mind when they conclude that what we call postmodern conspiracism reflects the cynicism and impoverishment of our troubled times. Postmodern conspiracism is the medium of hollowed-out men with no core. As Muirhead and Rosenblum lament: "The new conspiracism is politically sterile. It is de all the way down: destabilizing, degrading, deconstructing, and finally delegitimizing, without a constructive impulse."[61]

Notes

1 Russell Muirhead and Nancy Rosenblum, *A Lot of People Are Saying*, Kindle edition (Princeton: Princeton University Press, 2019) Location 85.
2 *en.oxforddictionaries.com/definition/conspiracism*.
3 We profited from our correspondence with Muirhead.
4 Muirhead and Rosenblum, *A Lot of People Are Saying*, Location 102.

5 *The Protocols of the Elders of Zion* is supposedly an anonymous account of a Zionist plans for world domination. However, as we'll see, those publicizing the document of contested origins—everyone from Russian mystic Sergei Nilus to industrialist Henry Ford—sought acclaim by revealing clandestine Jewish malevolence. Even now, the forgery is cited as evidence of a Jewish conspiracy.

6 Ted Goertzel, "The Conspiracy Theory Pyramid Scheme," Chpt. 15, in *Conspiracy Theories and the People Who Believe Them*, Kindle Edition, ed. Joseph E. Uscinski (London and New York: Oxford University Press, 2019).

7 Quoted by Ibid.

8 See "The Ford Pinto Cover-Up," *Mother Jones*, September/October 1977, accessed April 30, 2021, https://www.motherjones.com › uploads › v2n8.

9 Goertzel, "The Conspiracy Theory Pyramid Scheme," p. 226. We warn beginning logic students against such fallacious reasoning: E.g., Hitler got haircuts; Bernie gets haircuts, therefore …? Logicians will recognize this as "the fallacy of the undistributed middle term."

10 "Presidential Apology for the Study at Tuskegee," accessed May 27, 2012, Britannica, www.britannica.com.

11 Alexsandar Mishkov, "False Conspiracy Theory Turned Out to be True," accessed May 21, 2021, https://www.documentarytube.com/articles/tuskegee -experiment-fatal-conspiracy-theory-turned-out-to-be-truth. Also see the official CDC account of the study accessed May 21, 2021, https://www.cdc.gov /tuskegee/timeline.htm. As we write, certain scientists entertain a hypothesis about the origin of the Covid 19 virus: Did Chinese officials conspire to cover up a malfunction in the Wuhan Virology Lab? See Nicholas Wade, "The Origin of COVID: Did People or Nature Open Pandora's Box at Wuhan?" *The Bulletin of the Atomic Scientists*, May 5, 2021. President Biden ordered an investigation.

12 See Michael Albert's interview with Chomsky in *Peace Research* 35, no. 1 (May 2003): pp. 51–60.

13 See Fred Kaplan, "What's Really in the Downing Street Memos," *Slate*, June 15, 2005, accessed July 13, 2021, https://slate.com/news-and-politics/2005/06/ what-s-really-in-the-downing-street-memos.html.

14 Charles Pigden, "Everyone's a Conspiracy Theorist," in Richard Greene (ed.) *Conspiracy Theories: Philosophers Connect the Dots* (Chicagao: Open Court Publishing. 2020), p. 28.

15 Rob Brotherton, *Suspicious Minds: Why We Believe Conspiracy Theories* (London: Bloomsbury Sigma, 2017), p. 58.

16 See, for example, Joseph E. Uscinski and Joseph M. Parent, *American Conspiracy Theories* (Oxford, New York: Oxford University Press, 2014). The authors conducted what they call "extensive and exhausting" survey research to determine susceptibility to conspiracism. The study relied upon a national survey, coding thousands of letters to the editor, and Internet samples. The results are informative and of heuristic value. The dated study fails to give appropriate weight to transgressive Internet sites in promoting conspiracism and inspiring violence.

17 Katherine E. Hoffman, "Culture as Text: Hazards and Possibilities of Geertz' Literal/Literary Metaphor," *The Journal of North African Studies* 14, No. 3/4 (September/December 2009): p. 417. George Lakoff's *Metaphors We Live By* (Chicago: University of Chicago Press, 2003) offers a penetrating and accessible introduction to the role of metaphors in the construction of social reality. Victor Turner's *Drama, Fields and Metaphors: Symbolic Action in Human*

Society (Ithaca and London: Cornell University Press, 1974) offers a telling account of the role of metaphors in the enactment and remembrance of momentous events.

18 While it sounds like a bad marriage, the notion of action at a distance has implications for our study: Conspiracists attribute seemingly magical powers to a cabal of international Jews and to the Muslim Brotherhood. Somehow a cabal or brotherhood manages everyday life and orchestrates world-historical events—revolutions and wars. But how do they do it? Ironically, at this all-important juncture, conspiracists don't "connect the dots." How do historically oppressed, marginalized minorities manage to run the world? Action at a distance remains a mystery in conspiratorial theology.

19 Alyssa Weiner, "Global Trends in Conspiracy Theories Linking Jews with Coronavirus," in *AJC (American Jewish Community Newsletter)*, May 1, 2020, accessed September 6, 2022, https://www.ajc.org/news/global-trends-in-conspiracy-theories-linking-jews-with-coronavirus.

20 David Luban, "Hannah Arendt Meets QAnon: Conspiracy, Ideology, and the Collapse of Common Sense," *Georgetown University Law Center*, 2021, p. 20, accessed September 6, 2021, https.//scholarship.law.georgetown.edu/facpub /2384. We're indebted to Luban for his careful analysis and penetrating insights.

21 John Earnest Manifesto.

22 Luban, "Hannah Arendt Meets QAnon." Chapter 4 probes deeper into the role of website affiliation in promoting stigmatizing and violence.

23 Bat Ye'or, *Eurabia: The Euro-Arab Axis* (Madison: Fairleigh Dickinson University Press, 2005), p. 26.

24 Writing in *The Guardian* (May 7, 2016) University of Pennsylvania professor Guido Menzio indicates he was removed from a commercial flight and interviewed by the FBI when the passenger beside him became suspicious as he wrote differential equations. Accessed August 30, 2021, https://www.theguardian.com/us-news/2016/may/07/professor-flight-delay-terrorism-equation-american-airlines. "The Project" will be analyzed in more detail in Chapter Three.

25 Accessed in *Goodreads Quotes*, August 29, 2021, https://www.goodreads.com/ author/quotes/349707.Karl_Popper.

26 Nicholas Reimann, "QAnon Marked Friday As Trump 'Reinstatement' Day--Here Are Other Flop Predictions Of Trump's Return," *Forbes*, August 13, 2021, accessed August 30, 2021, https://www.forbes.com › nicholasreimann.

27 Brian L. Keeley, "Of Conspiracy Theory," *The Journal of Philosophy* 96, no. #3 (March 1999): 120; we're indebted to Keeley's insightful contrast between scientific and conspiracy theory.

28 Those concerned about the active QAnon imagination can read more in Bill McEwen, "Have You Heard the One About Biden's Face on Trump's Body?" *GV Wire*, January 22, 2021, accessed September 9, 2021, https://gvwire.com /2021/01/22/have-you-heard-the-one-about-bidens-face-on-trumps-body.

29 Brotherton, Location 910, Bloomsbury Sigma.

30 Ibid., Location 1219. Chapter 4 tortures a medical analogy: Vigorously attacking a conspiracy gone viral provokes a cytokine storm—overreaction to criticism that makes matters worse—may provoke violence.

31 Uscinski, *Conspiracy Theories and the People Who Believe Them*, p. 40.

32 Glenn Bezalel, "Conspiracy Theories and Religion: Reframing Conspiracy Theories as Bliks," *Episteme* 18 (2021): pp. 674–692.

33 Bradley Franks and Adrian Bangerter, "Conspiracy Theories as Quasi-Religious Mentality: An Integrated Account from Cognitive Science, Social Representation Theory, and Frame Theory," *Frontiers in Psychology,* July 16, 2003, p. 4.

34 See Steven T. Katz's account of secular religion in *The Paranoid Apocalypse: A Hundred Year Perspective on the Protocols of the Elders of Zion,* ed. Richard Landes and Steven T. Katz (New York and London: New York University Press, 2012.), p. 106. [Hereafter referred to as *Protocols.*]

35 Robert Brotherton and Silan Eser, "Bored to Fears: Boredom Proneness, Paranoia, and Conspiracy Theories," *Personality and Individual Difference* 80 (2015): 2. As the title suggests, the authors want to give boredom the appropriate place in a concatenated account of susceptibility to conspiracism. Despite its limitations (small sampling and location), we believe the study has heuristic value.

36 "The Schizotypal Personality Disorder," accessed August 27, 2022, https://www.mayoclinic.org/diseases-conditions/schizotypal-personality-disorder/symptoms-causes/syc-20353919.

37 Neil Postman, *Amusing Ourselves to Death: Public Discourse in the Age of Show Business* (New York: Penguin, 1985).

38 Jan-Willem Prooijen, Joline Ligthart, Sabine Rosema, and Yang Xu, "The Entertainment Value of Conspiracy Theories," *British Journal of Psychology* 113 (February 2022): pp. 25–48, accessed August 27, 2022, https://resolver.scholarsportal.info/resolve/00071269/v113i0001/25_tevoct.xml.

39 Ron joined a "Next Door Neighbor" site in San Diego and got local gossip, amusing cat photos, and pleas to find lost dogs. He did not expect neighbors to form a group entitled "It's OK to be White." This White Supremacy-lite clique celebrated the marvels of their pigmentation—or lack therefore—while disparaging people of color. Ron congratulated his neighbors for choosing their parents carefully.

40 As we'll see, certain conspiracists claim that perfidious Jewish and Muslim secret schemes were both "stumbled upon" at various times in Switzerland with the discovery of the *Protocols* and its doppelganger, "The Project."

41 Tarrant's Manifesto, "The Great Replacement," accessed November 8, 2019, https://www.bing.com/videos/search?q=tarrant+manifesto%2c+the+great+replacement&&view=detail&mid=8FF4.

42 Luban, "Hannah Arendt Meets QAnon," p. 8.

43 It seems that Masons are no longer in vogue among conspiracists. At one time this order was considered a tool of perfidious Jews. These days discussing conspiracies hatched at a Masonic lodge are as ludicrous as attributing murderous schemes to the Rotary Club.

44 See Pew Forum, accessed September 20, 2012, estimate of Muslim population: https://www.pewresearch.org/fact-tank/2018/01/03/new-estimates-show-u-s-muslim-population-continues-to-grow/; estimate of Jewish population: https://www.pewforum.org/2021/05/11/the-size-of-the-u-s-jewish-population.

45 Norman Cohn, The *Pursuit of the Millennium* (Fairhaven: Essential Books, 1957), p. 17.

46 Whether Spencer's "Alt.Right" is a Rebranded Nazi Movement is controversial. While Spencer does not publicly advocate genocide, his Nazi-style saluting at a Trump rally leaves an indelible impression.

47 "Richard Bertram Spencer," *Southern Poverty Law Center,* accessed September 22, 2021, https://www.splcenter.org/fighting-hate/extremist-files/individual/richard-bertrand-spencer-0.

48 Julia Bell, *Radical Attention* (London: Peninsula Press, 2020), 47.
49 "Jean-François Lyotard," in the *Internet Encyclopedia*, accessed September 27, 2012, https://iep.utm.edu › lyotard.
50 Muirhead and Rosenblum, *A Lot of People are Saying*, Location 604.
51 Ibid., Location 176.
52 "Beavis and Butt-Head," *Wikipedia*, accessed September 24, 2021, https://en.wikipedia.org/wiki/Beavis_and_Butt-Head.
53 "The Great Replacement," Brenton Tarrant's Manifesto.
54 Angela Nagle, *Kill All Normies* (Alresford, Hants: Zero Books, 2017).
55 Ibid., p. 14.
56 See Mike Rothschild's account of QAnon in his *Into the Storm* (Brooklyn: Melville Publishing, 2021). The author hastens to mention that he is not related to the Rothschild banking families—a perennial target of conspiracist accusations.
57 Muirhead and Rosenblum, *A Lot of People are Saying*, Location 109.
58 Gwen Farrell, "What's Going One?" Quoted in *Eve*, May 20, 2022, accessed September 6, 2022, https://www.eviemagazine.com/post/57-people-from-bill-and-hillary-clintons-inner-circle-died-strange-circumstances.
59 Ibid., p. 9. Ron first encountered the lulz in the 1960s reading the *Berkeley Barb's* contest to guess the date of the death of Mamie Eisenhower.
60 See, for example, "The Most Controversial Memes of All Times," accessed September 27, 2021, https://www.youtube.com/watch?v=4PGs-gJMvQI.
61 Muirhead and Rosenblum, *A Lot of People are Saying*, Location 176.

2 Long Ago in a Prague Cemetery Far Away

> When talk turns to worldwide conspiracies, the long shadow of the "Protocols of the Learned Elders of Zion," … can never be far away. Donald J. Trump said his Democratic opponent, Hillary Clinton, "meets in secret with international banks to plot the destruction of U.S. sovereignty in order to enrich these global financial powers."[1]

The Trump presidency was a dark time. Conspiracism, no longer the refuge of losers, became the vernacular of winners. Was Trump a true believer or just an opportunist pandering to those convinced that malevolent forces plot against them—both perhaps? In any case, despite his daughter's conversion to Judaism, he resorted to Judeophobic "dog whistles" about international bankers and other globalists. Jewish financier George Soros got blamed for sponsoring a Central American "invasion" of the United States, and Trump supporters even claimed that Soros supplied bricks for an American-style *kristallnacht* during civil rights protests—a despicable charge to levy against a Jew who fled Nazi terror.

Would Trump have been more enlightened had the *Protocols* never appeared? The dark shadow, of course, did not originate with him nor with the *Protocols* itself—the document certainly did not eclipse millennia of enlightened discourse and policy regarding Jews. This novel document does not merely assert the existence of a Jewish conspiracy; those with a will to believe take it as *proof* of such malevolent plans. We're offered, in effect, a ringside seat to a secret Zionist convocation. We can read for ourselves the Senior Elder's report on the status of the conspiracy and imminent plans for world domination—at the terrible expense of the Gentiles.[2] Conspiracy theorists who—despite evidence to the contrary—endorse the *Protocols'* authenticity ignore the *real* conspiracy: fabricating and promoting a forgery designed to inflame hatred and fear of the Jewish people. On rare occasions, when they entertain the possibility of forgery, they reassure skeptics that God reveals terrible truths in mysterious ways.

DOI: 10.4324/9781003207894-2

We turn to the *Protocols*[3] not merely because it is recommended and read: This eerie compendium of Jew hatred is sold at Walmart and promoted as a not-to-be-missed bargain on Amazon—"Protocol of Zion on Amazon—Low Priced." We revisit the fabrication because it provides a window through which we gaze upon that long, deep shadow cast by the imagined, abstract Jew. Not surprisingly, seen in its historical context, the text reflected the prevailing antisemitic zeitgeist—a response to the discontents of modernity—a malaise (like much else) blamed on the Jews. However, the *Protocols* is derivative: a variation on a perennial theme scaffolded on plagiarized, 19th-century novels.

We interpret the theme in a Janus-like perspective—a conduit of hate and paranoia linking the past and the future. The forgers gazed backward and absorbed and valorized millennia of Jew hatred and paranoia. They looked forward to persecuting Jews; whether they saw their efforts as a "warrant for genocide" is arguable. However, the work seemed destined for Russia and Eastern Europe—*a warrant for pogroms*. The 1903 Russian score orchestrates these fictions into 24 movements—music to Jew haters' ears—a requiem for Gentiles and for European civilization itself. Historian Johannes Heil recognizes the never-ending theme. Medieval fantasies are sustained and reinforced by revealing the terrifying machinations of an international, Jewish cabal and by dehumanizing Jews themselves, reducing diverse, disputatious people to a singular, metastasizing organism.[4]

We present a synopsis of the *Protocols*. Perhaps, as *Guardian* columnist David Baddiel quips, a single phrase might do: "Short of a conspiracy theory? You can always blame the Jews."[5] The synopsis raises further issues:

- How did the *Protocols* originate? No one seems to know for sure.
- Why then do most scholars concur—it's a forgery?
- Is the *Protocols* a response to the discontents of modernity—a rhetorical question.
- And what of its afterlife? Like the vampires of the 19th-century imagination, it won't die. It lives on in the Jew hatred in *The Turner Diaries* and haunts an interactive fantasy game known as QAnon.[6] Finally, who could have known that this elaborate plagiarism, informed by 19th-century novels would be dismembered into the vile shards and transgressive memes that besmirch the postmodern Internet?

A Preface to the *Protocols*

The Protocols is the most famous anti-Semitic tract in the western world, and though it's regularly referenced … I've never met anyone who has read it … I suspect the vast majority of people who have referenced it have not read it.[7]

We read it. Its prefatory commentaries are as revealing and harrowing as the document itself. Henry Ford gave Texe Marrs—author of a series of books that purportedly expose the malevolent machinations of various secret societies—the honor of penning the foreword to his edition; Marrs can't say enough about its significance:

> [It] may well be the most important book you have ever read. The Protocols of the Learned Elders of Zion is more than a book ... It is nothing less than a blueprint by a moneyed and privileged elite ... to subjugate the entire world ... a prescription for mass murder and genocide on a scale unparalleled in the annals of human history.[8]

Today, Marrs might charitably be called "tone deaf." The term "genocide" (unknown when his commentary was originally published by Ford in 1934) was coined in 1948 by Raphael Lemkin, a Jew who fled the Nazis. The volume was revised in 2011. Evidently Marrs, or another, inserted the term in the revised edition—long after the Nazi-perpetrated genocide.

Ford himself, however, was not tone deaf regarding the antisemitic zeitgeist—he heard it loud and clear—as do we. As he wrote in one of his newspaper columns: "To openly use the word 'Jew,' or to expose it nakedly to print, is somehow improper."[9] Even now, the unvarnished invocation "Jew" seems derogatory. "Jew" used as an adjective, noun, or verb has a distinctly pejorative ring. Contrast "that Irishman Donovan living down the street," with "that Jew Goldstein living down the street." Or contrast, "He's a Jew" with "He's Norwegian." And how many times have we heard "Being Jewed-down"? Better to deal with an honest "Yankee trader"—who always looks out for you. Sensitive to pejorative connotations, public discourse softens the abrasive "Jew" with "Jewish person." Ford and latter-day antisemites deem pejorative connotations appropriate.

John Wayne v. Shylock

Ford himself instructs the reader on the respective racial traits of Jew and Gentile, for Jews are not simply members of another religion; they are another race—a distinctive other. Biology is destiny—John Wayne isn't Shylock. Unlike the Jew, the quintessential Gentile is "slow, honest, plain-spoken and straight-dealing." No wonder the cunning, quick-witted Jew shamelessly outsmarts such guileless innocence. (No doubt the Gentile captains of industry frequenting Ford's exclusive city club shunned the very thought of taking advantage of anyone.) By way of contrast, the "international Jew," bereft of Ford's imagined Protestant humility, is megalomaniacal. The craven Jewish race craves world control; indeed, this perfidious race *already* wields too much control—they're doing what comes naturally. Ford asserts that Jews themselves are aware of the inherent dishonesty of their race. "This [unscrupulous racial] type does not grow anywhere other than on a Jewish stem."[10]

As Ford continues to draw such distinctions, it begins to appear that not only do Jews and Gentiles represent different races, they are different species. Ford's depiction of the Jew reminds us of bygone Hollywood depictions of alien invaders from toxic planets with orange skies and robots on the march. Like these Saturday matinee alien invaders, Ford's Jew possesses remarkable knowledge of human nature, history, and statecraft— to say nothing of the race's uncanny powers: "dazzling in its brilliant completeness, and terrible in the objects to which it turns its powers."[11]

We doubt that Ford derived this perspective solely from reading the *Protocols*. As *Washington Post* columnist A. James Rudin observes, Ford was in the thrall of prejudice before he encountered the *Protocols*. His paper, the *Dearborn Independent* purchased in 1919, highlighted years of bigotry: Notable headlines included "Prohibition-era whiskey nigger gin," and jazz—"Yiddish moron music."[12] We assume that the fabrication was an accelerant that reinforced preexisting antisemitism, not the cause. It seems unlikely that a single text could infect an otherwise tolerant mind with virulent bigotry.

True, facing bad press and litigation, Ford eventually apologized for his newspaper and previous publications. His regrets seem disingenuous; he claimed he was unfamiliar with the publications' contents. Ironically, he did not live to see the ascendancy of Mark Fields, an American Jew, who (in 2014) became president and CEO of Ford Motors.[13] Nevertheless, Ford's celebration of imagined racial purity and virtue is not forgotten. Former President Trump visited the Michigan factory in May 2020 and eulogized Ford's racial heritage: "The company was founded by … Henry Ford. Good bloodlines, good bloodlines, if you believe in that stuff you've got good blood."[14]

On Reading the *Protocols*

We expected the *Protocols* would be a cross between a neo-Nazi diatribe and slurs scrawled on a men's room wall. However, the document is not stupid or outlandish; on the contrary, it begins with an unremarkable recitation of a theme familiar to students of politics: political realism—no more shocking than reading Machiavelli. In Protocol 1 the Senior Elder—the sole voice in the document—channels the Florentine iconoclast when he reminds the convocation that: "Men with bad instincts are more in number than the good …. Governing them are [*sic*] attained by violence and terrorization."[15] He warns that without absolute despotism there is no governance, let alone civilization.

In what, no doubt, alarms those who take the fabrication seriously, the Elder boasted that "Our [Jewish] kingdom will be ... a despotism of such magnificent proportions as to be ... in a position to wipe out the goyim who oppose us by deed or word."[16] Cruel statecraft attains its apotheosis in Protocol 10 as the Elder vows vengeance. No longer sheep, Jews become wolves. "The goyim are a flock of sheep, and we are their wolves. And you know what happens when the wolves get hold of the flock?"[17] Many will perish, of course, but we must know that "Each victim on our side is worth in the sight of God a thousand goyim."[18]

The Elders will stop at nothing to have their way with Christian civilization. They will persist in corrupting the youth and disrupting and demoralizing the established order. Indeed, they are not above placing "our women in the places of dissipation frequented by the goyim." Minds too will be dissipated by the works of Darwin, Marx, and Nietzsche—sponsored somehow by the Jewish cabal. (Why Jews sponsored Nietzsche—an ardent critic of Judaism—is not explained.)

The Elder urged that most men *do* live by bread alone. In Hobbes' view, life is "short, nasty, and brutish"—without absolute monarchy. The Elder, bent upon world-class domination, insisted that life must become short, nasty, and brutish—for the goyim—*with* monarchy. Exercising absolute control of the economy, the Jews will induce shortages in essential items, lower wages, and higher prices. Only then, impoverished, corrupt, and dissolute, will hapless Gentiles "drop their hands in despairing impotence ... drop down before us, if for no other reason but ... the right to exist."[19]

According to the Elder, Jews already control the world's money and media, happy days are *almost* here again—for no one but the Jews. As he boasts: "The weapons in our hands are limitless ambitions, burning greediness, merciless vengeance, hatred and malice." The mob, we are told, will love the Jew's display of brute force—they always have. And so, as we learn in the final Protocol, the King of the Jews—*the* planetary potentate—will emerge from the House of David. A glorious despot (who unlike David himself) will be uncorrupted by sensual passion. The Elder concludes that he has carefully depicted the secrets of the past, present, and future of God's Chosen People.

Origins

Throughout history Jews prayed that others would simply let them be. Who decided to channel the antisemitic zeitgeist, purloin two novels, and forge this notorious document? The title of historian Richard Levy's research is telling: "*Setting the Record Straight Regarding the Protocols of the Elders of Zion: A Fool's Errand?*" However, rather than a fool's errand, "setting the record straight" became a distinguished scholars' errand. Speculation about authorship is a cottage industry that immerses inquiry in contested accounts of baroque intrigues, exegetical conundrums, and ineffectual litigation.

Esther Webman is among the scholars who realize that attempts to locate authorship must be tempered by a caveat: "It is still not certain who wrote this antisemitic pamphlet, but the evidence suggests that it was cobbled together from pre-existing sources by ... the Russian secret police."[20] In his influential *Warrant for Genocide,* Norman Cohn is sympathetic to this account; even so, he notes the difficulties inherent in detecting the origins of the forgery. "In trying to unravel the early history of the *Protocols* one comes up against ambiguities, uncertainties, riddles." Nevertheless, he concludes the text was forged by Pyotr Ivanovich Rachkovsky, a Russian secret police agent.[21] The controversy continues. Historian Michael Hagemeister's research casts doubt upon Cohn's conclusion: Perhaps he gave too much credence to testimony at the Berne Trial. Others speculate about the *Protocols*' French origins. Casting doubt upon such speculation, literary scholar Cesare G. De Michelis locates the document's inception back in Czarist Russia in the aftermath of a Russian Zionist congress in September 1902. Originally a parody on Jewish idealism. Not unlike ironic attempts at humor on the postmodern Internet, the attempted parody was taken seriously and circulated among notorious antisemites. De Michelis contends that the text's initial publisher deliberately obscured the satirical origins of the text and lied about it in the decades afterward.[22]

Suffice it to conclude that the text's origins remain clouded in controversy and mystery.[23] Decades of speculation have passed: No authoritative tribunal will settle the matter anytime soon. It would be audacious for us to suggest that we can resolve the dispute. However, what is salient is not controversial: Noteworthy litigation corroborated allegation of forgery; most significant—the discovery of the plagiarizing and paraphrasing of two 19th-century novels is certainly telling. In any case, the *Protocols*' influence is of more concern than its dubious origins. As Hannah Arendt averred long ago, what is relevant is not: "to prove ... what the whole world already knows and that we are dealing with a forgery, but to explain why such a blatant forgery is still believed by so many."[24]

Fabrication

According to Cohn, Sergei Nilus (who edited and promoted the forgery) made a damaging admission to his skeptical French acquaintance, Count Alexandre du Chayla:

Let us admit that the Protocols are a forgery. Cannot God make use of a forgery in order to illuminate the iniquity of what is about to occur? Cannot God, in response to our faith, transform the bones of a dog into the relics of a miracle? He can thus place into the mouth of a liar the annunciation of truth.[25]

Cohn depicts Nilus as a character out of central casting: "Truly a Russian type, big and strong, with a grey beard and deep eyes ... He wore boots, and a Russian shirt with a belt with a prayer embroidered on it."[26] Early in life, we are told, Nilus sank into the depths of nihilism. He was enthralled by Nietzsche's ruminations. We imagine him beside the Teutonic professor staring into the abyss—as the abyss stares back. The mystic's biography bespeaks of what we've called "the dialectic of despair": The deeper the despair, the more soaring the rebounding fanaticism. An epiphany lifted Nilus to manic heights as he read the *Protocols*—surely an omen of the advent of the Jewish Antichrist.

As Cohn quips: "In ... pages which deserve to be in any anthology of religious eccentricity, [Nilus' friend Alexandre] du Chayla has shown just what the *Protocols* meant to its most celebrated editor."[27] Like any conspiracy theologian worthy of his paranoia, Nilus expected his aristocratic friend would be awestruck as he unveiled the text's newly discovered, shocking revelations. Listening to most harrowing passages du Chayla was neither awestruck nor dumbfounded. The aristocrat's profound indifference offers a felicitous lesson in confronting conspiracists: His friend didn't attack Nilus personally, mock the *Protocols*' patent absurdity, nor question the putative evidence. And yet, his response couldn't have been more devastating—it deprived Nilus of oxygen so to speak. Blasé, distracted by other matters—du Chayla had no interest in arguing with Nilus. *He told Nilus that he had heard this story before* [Ital. ours]. Crestfallen, Nilus insisted that his friend must carefully read the document for himself.

The mystic crossed himself three times before an icon of Mary and solemnly intoned "Here it is ... the charter of the Kingdom of the Anti-Christ." Du Chayla (perhaps out of friendship or uncommon courtesy) took two and a half hours to read the text; Nilus eagerly awaited his verdict: "*I told him straight out ... I don't believe in the Elders of Zion*" [ital. ours]. Nilus felt betrayed and diminished by his longtime friend who doubted his revelations; he accused him of being in league with the Devil: "Satan deceives people into denying his influence, indeed, his very existence."[28]

This insinuation may have ended their friendship, for du Chayla testified against his old friend at litigation contesting the document's authenticity—the Berne Trial. In any case du Chayla feared for his friend's sanity. Conspiracists can abide accusations of fraud and shoddy logic. Indeed, they thrive on it—they relish being taken seriously. But they cannot countenance profound indifference; it may drive them mad. It appeared that Nilus' fanaticism brought him perilously close to the edge of the abyss once again:

> I felt ... fear. It was nearly midnight. The gaze, the voice, the reflex-like gestures—everything about Nilus gave me the feeling that we were walking on the edge of an abyss and that at any moment his reason might disintegrate into madness.[29]

Litigation

Turning briefly to the litigation, most notably, the Berne Trial of 1935. There was good news and bad news for The Swiss Federation of Jewish Communities' suit against local Nazi sympathizers. The Federation claimed the sympathizers (supported by the German government) were distributing a slanderous forgery—the *Protocols*. The presiding justice, Walter Meyer, agreed:

> He hoped there will come a time when no one will any longer comprehend how in the year 1935 almost a dozen fully sensible and reasonable men could for fourteen days torment their brains before a court of Berne over the authenticity or lack of authenticity of these so-called Protocols, these Protocols that, for all the harm they have already caused and may yet cause, are nothing but ridiculous nonsense.[30]

An appellate court overturned the verdict on a technicality: The Federation based its case on obscenity statutes. The court deemed the text fraudulent but not obscene. However, more recent hearings also indicted the document as a forgery to no avail. In 1964 the United States Senate Judiciary Committee concluded that those who peddle the fabricated *Protocols* spread hate and dissension among the public. (Hate and dissension were its main attraction.) In 1993 a Moscow trial, also an extremist organization, was found guilty of fraud for promoting the text.[31]

However, we find the research of Philip Graves and Norman Cohn more compelling than the unimpressive outcomes results of litigation—at least for those willing to entertain the possibility of fraud. Cohn cites a May 1920 issue of the *London Times* in which alarmed editorial writers took the recently trans-lated *Protocols*' seriously: "Have we ... escaped a 'Pax Germanica' only to fall into a 'Pax Judaeica'?" According to Cohn, a *Times* correspondent (Philip Graves) inadvertently came across Maurice Joly's novel and noted the blatant plagiarism: Graves compared Joly's 1864 satire, *Enfers entre Montesquieu et Marchievel*[32] (*Dialogue between Montesquieu and Machiavelli in Hell*), with the 1920 English translation of the *Protocols*. He discovered that "There are scores of ... parallels between the books. Fully 50 paragraphs in the Protocols are simply paraphrases of passages in the Dialogues."[33]

The Jew as Machiavelli

In the imaginary dialog Montesquieu expresses Enlightenment liberalism—buoyant optimism about the human condition and the prospects for a better world. Not surprisingly, the Florentine dominates the dialog—the voice of amoral realpolitik. In this not-so-subtle satire, Machiavelli becomes Napoleon III's avatar: icy-cold, calculating opportunism personified—contempt for the masses and the celebration of gratuitous violence. The censors caught on; Joly was imprisoned. But Joly didn't have Jews in mind; those who forged the *Protocols* did—the Senior Elder, as we've seen, reiterates Machiavelli's jaundiced view of human nature. Graves urged: "Read this book through and you will find irrefutable proof that the *Protocols* ... is a plagiarism."

The *Times* took note, admitted its mistake, and featured this headline on August 13, 1921:

The Truth about "The Protocols": A LITERARY FORGERY[34]

Cohn found the *Protocols* trafficking in another 19th-century novel penned by Hermann Goedsche. The author, according to Cohn, was a minor official in the German postal service who lost his post for promoting forged documents. He turned his efforts to maligning Jews in his novel *Biarritz*. The work, no doubt, would remain in well-deserved obscurity if a chapter entitled "In the Jewish Cemetery in Prague" hadn't become the *Protocols*' template. Goedsche's attempt at a Gothic novella reads like a rejected script for a low-budget Halloween production—his imagery was already trite in 1868.

As the story unfolds, a secret nocturnal cabal enters the cemetery through creaking gates and pays homage to a sacred tombstone: "A clock strikes midnight .... A blue flame appears ... A hollow voice says. 'I greet you heads of the twelve tribes of Israel.' [The assembled Elders reply], 'We greet you son of the accursed.'" The Jews count their gold, boast of their control of commerce, and vow to totally control the press. However, these practices are but means to an end—world domination. They vow that the sword of Israel will vanquish enemies, and when their descendants meet a hundred years hence, Jews will enjoy heaven on earth. Cohn suggests that Jew haters had a robust appetite for this 1868 tawdry literature—they took it seriously.[35] The cemetery fugue epitomizes the transition from the medieval, demonic Jew, to the despised international Jew of modernity. However, remnants of the medieval superstition remain as the Elders practice black magic and worship a Golden calf. But Shylock emerges in the garments of modern industry and commerce.

Hearing Voices

Historian Richard Landes deems the *Protocols* fraudulent because: "The voice of the Elders was not a recognizably Jewish voice." (We didn't realize there was such a voice, a voice that spoke for an entire, factious people; is there also a "Jewish gaze"?) True, his stereotyping is generous, albeit chauvinistic: Jews, according to Landes, eschew realpolitik in favor of high ideals—but Jews are *too* good for their own good. Indeed, they are overly critical of themselves. Landes warns fellow Jews to watch what they say— lest ever-attentive Arab enemies take advantage of such self-critical candor.

Not adverse to constructing an other himself, Landes hears cruel and cunning Gentile voices, the bravado of coldly calculating realists: "The irony here is that the 'higher truth' of what the text [*Protocols*] embodies is not about the Jews but about this particularly powerful strand of [repugnant] Gentile political thought."[36] Apparently, Jews and Gentiles are different species. He hears the dissonant sounds of another species in the cacophony of Gentile voices: Thrasymachus arguing that "might makes right" [in Plato's *Republic*]; Carolingian lords pillaging Europe; the German aristocracy "pruning back" troublesome peasantry. Above the din he hears Machiavelli loud and clear—not a Jewish voice.[37] Realpolitik is anathema to naively idealistic Jews.

This would be news to Palestinians who hear the strident voice of Israeli realpolitik as Israeli Defense Forces keep them in their place by "cutting the grass"—bombing Palestinian resistance in the occupied territories. Arab translations of the *Protocols* are held responsible for inciting violence against Israelis. Apparently, if not for this document, Palestinians would have been content to become refugees in 1948 and wouldn't object to their current immiseration in Gaza. The tattered *Protocols* text supposedly promotes widespread Muslim perfidy: The Muslim Brotherhood allegedly uses the text as a guide to their conquest of Europe.[38]

The Discontents of Modernity

The origins of the *Protocols* remain "clouded in mystery"; even so, the fabrication bears the indelible signature of the discontents of modernity. The concept of "modernity" itself encompasses a broad sweep in the history of ideas and institutional practices. In his penetrating exploration of the subject, political scientist Steven B. Smith begins by emphasizing the complexities and far-reaching implications of the advent of modernity—as he suggests, perhaps "modernities" might be apt. And yet, he points to a common denominator—*a break with tradition*.[39] In order to grasp the context that gave rise to the *Protocols*, we concern ourselves with two seemingly unrelated breaks: the advent of cosmology of modern science and the emancipation of the Jews. We see these breaks as displacements: Humanity got evicted from the center of the universe; worse yet, Jews weren't kept in their place.

In the world according to Copernican revolutionaries the cosmos no longer revolved around our irredeemably narcissistic selves—it never had. Against our will and behind our backs we were thrown into a world profoundly indifferent to our needs and purposes. Nietzsche bore witness to this erasure of our horizon. Darkness fell. His Zarathustra proclaimed the death of God. (Given the news, a student allowed that she didn't even know He was sick.) Philosopher of science, E. A. Burtt related this insult to human aspirations and self-esteem:

> Purposeless ... void of meaning, is the world which Science presents for our belief .... [Man's] origin, his growth, his hopes and fears, his loves and his beliefs, are but the outcome of accidental collocations of atoms; that no fire, no heroism, no intensity of thought and feeling, can preserve an individual life beyond the grave.[40]

A Catholic theologian echoed Romantic Era poets (and perhaps many of us) as he wistfully longs for a bygone enchanted world, a realm redolent with mystery and magic; like William Blake, he would awaken us from the mechanistic world of "Newton's sleep."

> Why wouldn't we long for the place where God is alive and magic afoot ... I would dwell where the dragons are, where the Grail is sought, where prayer is efficacious, where the stones cry out, where miracles are so common ... where human life is thick and rich and sacramental.[41]

Deaf to such idyllic "sermons in stone," those who forged the *Protocols* reenchanted the world with a horror show, not magical arcadian days. The forgers, whoever they were, reenchanted the void with a hateful Manichean immorality play. The usual supernatural cast was replaced by this-worldly Jewish actors: Satan reappeared as the Senior Elder as his minions corrupted hallowed traditions.

The center didn't hold: Jews no longer knew their place. The ghettos opened, and Jews were afforded a modicum of civil rights: some assimilated, and a few attained success in the professions of science, finance, and industry. As journalist Michael Goldfarb comments: "The story of Jewish emancipation is not just about a religious minority's struggles to integrate, it is about a group regarded as an ethnic and racial minority fighting for its place in society."[42] Stunning stories of Jewish achievement shocked the established system as Jews profaned sacred Gentile spaces. Goldfarb continues: "Now everything was changing fast ... Benjamin Disraeli would become one of the great men of this new era, first as a popular novelist, then as British prime minister."[43]

Predictably, the Jewish Prime Minister encountered hostility. A member of parliament chided: "Sir. You will die on the gallows or of some unspeakable disease." Disraeli didn't let the insult pass: "That depends, sir, on whether I embrace your policies or your mistress."[44] Disraeli wisely counseled, "Hope for the best, but prepare for the worst." The worst happened to an emancipated French officer.

Alfred Dreyfus didn't know his place. He personified the essence of modernity—breaking with tradition. In 1894 this French Army captain, of Jewish heritage, was falsely convicted of treason—selling secrets to the Germans. He personified the treachery attributed to the emancipated Jew, "who is everywhere but belongs nowhere,"—a slogan of the time. Upon his conviction, cheered on by antisemites, the Jewish officer was humiliated amid ceremonial savoir-faire: "His insignia medals were stripped from him, his sword was broken over the knee of the degrader, and he was marched around the grounds in his ruined uniform to be jeered and spat at, while piteously declaring his innocence and his love of France."[45]

New evidence came to light: Apparently, a Major Estherhazy was the real culprit—but the evidence was suppressed. However, after enduring nearly five years on Devil's Island, Dreyfus was retried. Once again, was convicted with forged documents However, succumbing to considerable domestic and international outrage, he was eventually pardoned. Reinstated, Dreyfus fought for the French during World War I.

Antisemitism and Pseudoscience

> When Wilhelm Marr did coin it in 1879 ... it was *good* to be an antisemite, it was a matter of common sense (and in Marr's case, patriotism). This is not all that surprising, after all the second half of the nineteenth century was an age of extremism and racial paranoia.
>
> Reza Zia Ebrahimi[46]

Wilhelm Marr and Ernest Renan sought the imprimatur of science to valorize their biases. The imaginative hierarchies of pseudoscience put Jews and Muslims in their proper place. Marr and Renan embraced emerging pseudoscience to reenchant the world with a Manichean drama scripted in race and language. We do not know whether Marr and Renan viscerally hated Jews—how could we? They represented themselves as observers of the natural order. By way of a crude analogy: We know lions kill zebras, but we don't hate lions for doing what comes naturally. Likewise, Jews do what comes naturally—how could they not?

"Antisemitism" is a relatively new contribution to an ancient lexicon of prejudice and persecution. Wilhelm Marr coined the term to signify his essentialized phobia regarding the imagined "Semitic race." Not without reason Hebrew University's Moshe Zimmerman refers to Marr, a strident opponent of Jewish emancipation, as the very "patriarch of anti-Semitism"; he recognizes Marr's indelible influence.[47] Marr was not obsessed with the Jewish religion—just another Abrahamic faith as far as he was concerned. "Antisemitism" signified the racialization of Jews—ascribing an indelible essence. All Jews inherit the same deplorable traits, traits instantiated in the *Protocols* and the world according to Henry Ford. Jews were assimilating into German culture—precisely the problem as far as Marr was concerned. He would not be deceived: True to their nature, Jews conspired to destroy Germany from within.

Indebted to fashionable taxonomies of racial classification, Marr was neither the first nor the last to denigrate Jews as a malevolent race. However, rather than invoking the crudity of traditional Jew hatred, he invoked merging racist pseudoscience—its taxonomies gave an aura of respectable, carefully calibrated research. These classifications, of course, were not derived from genetic testing, nor were the metrics derived from carefully crafted historical or sociological studies—they were self-confessional. Somehow, classifiers invariably determined that *their* imagined race was the best.

Jews became an immutable other—another species. Just as a wolf in sheep's clothing is still a wolf, a Jew converting to Christianity is still a Jew with a unique propensity: The Jewish (Semitic) race is genetically bent upon the destruction of its hosts. No wonder wandering Jews are despised wherever the diaspora leads them. Never mind that there is no history of diaspora Jews attacking host nations—the obverse is true. According to the man who coined the term "anti-Semitism," perfidious Jews are particularly obsessed with destroying Aryans—not surprisingly, the highest-ranking race in many a pseudo-scientific classification. In Marr's paranoid vision, Jews were taking over and make no mistake: They were about to make Germany the "New Palestine" (i.e., the Jewish Homeland) of Europe. In 1879 he lamented that Jews had already triumphed in Germany. Jews enduring routine discrimination and suffering pograms were unaware of their triumphant ascendancy:

> I publicly proclaim the world-historical triumph of Jewry ... from feeble beginnings Jewry has grown beyond you [the German people]. It has corrupted society ... possesses the controlling position in commerce, infiltrates increasingly into state offices ... and has left you little more than the hard manual labor that it always despised.[48]

Apparently, not entirely convinced by his own alarmist rhetoric, he didn't abandon hope. He saw a glimmer of hope for renewed Aryan glory in a tract entitled *The Way to Victory of Germany over Judaism*. His fears inspired antisemitic leagues marching under the banner of the swastika. Historians mention that, late in life, Marr recanted some of his views. However, his initial, race-based Judeophobia left an indelible impression, not his second thoughts. His early views resonate in the *Protocols*, in extremist websites, and in the white supremacist terror plaguing Jewish communities.

Ironically, despite the concept's inglorious origins at the hands of the likes of Marr, there is virtually an unthought, unquestioned consensus within the Jewish community: "Antisemitism" applies to Jews and *only* to Jews. Never mind that not all Semites are Jews, and not all Jews are Semites. Historian Richard Levy was a rare academic who found "antisemitism" problematic: Not only is it a misnomer, "it gives continued life to a pernicious myth ... negative traits comprising a monolithic, Jewish essence."[49] Members of the Jewish community resent attempts to indict prejudice against Semitic Arabs as antisemitism. It's as if the term "antisemitism" is a precious heritage, a coinage first inscribed on parchment by Talmudic scholars in candlelit quarters in a medieval shtetl. The Jewish community has Wilhelm Marr to thank for its exclusive franchise, a man who tried to put Jews in their place.

Semites Need to Watch Their Language

Gil Hochberg, a UCLA comparative literature scholar, argues that: "Popular images of Jews and Muslims ... in Western media ironically echo nineteenth-century European depictions of Semites—both Jews and Muslims—as devoted monotheistic fanatics controlled by zeal and despotism and in need of external salvation."[50] The complicity of Western powers, namely Great Britain and the United States, in fomenting hostility between Jew and Arab is brushed aside with banalities: "They've been at each other's throats forever!"

According to Hochberg, Ernest Renan and other influential philologists interpreted Semitic languages in terms of highly imaginative meanings and deficits, and crowned their tendentious efforts with scientific status. They assumed that language is the very signature of a people's mentality and character: "The spirit of each people and its language are very closely connected, and language in turn ... serves as the limit of the spirit."[51] This circular reasoning, in effect, promotes racism without race, and prompted disparaging classifications in various taxonomies:

> To speak about ... Semitism in nineteenth-century Europe is to speak about a prevailing obsession with hierarchical classification .... [The] separation of people in the name of modern scientific knowledge into distinct civilizations.[52]

However, in Hochberg's view, 19th-century philology was a science in name only. Renan's claims about Semitic languages were not—as one would expect from a philologist—based upon a filigreed exegesis of texts nor more expansive hermeneutic inquiry. They were self-confessional. Philologists such as Renan were not disinterested scientists; they had an agenda: *demonstrating the superiority of what they understood as Aryan civilization.* Philology became a weaponized enterprise that "introduced, studied, and circulated [findings] to prove the linguistic, mental, religious, and cultural superiority of Christian Europe."[53]

Amid this anthem to white, European superiority, Semites—namely Jews and Arabs—got bad press: low ranking in the 19th-century penchant for classification. According to Renan and his followers, Semitic and Aryan languages reveal radically different mental capacities and innate sensibilities. The vastly superior Aryan languages are media of deep thought, robust, masculine philosophizing, and glorious myths—we can almost hear strains of Wagner's "Ride of the Valkyries." As Nietzsche averred in *The Birth of Tragedy*, the Semitic essence expresses an effeminate, servile mentality. However, the Aryan is guided by obdurate facts and by sturdy logic. (The Nazi era casts doubt upon celebrations of unfailing Teutonic rationality.) By way of contrast, the Semite believes and worships in tongues not fit for mythology, philosophy, or civil life. (The Old Testament is redolent with mythology, and somehow Renan and the others overlooked the rich heritage of Arabian myths and philosophy.)

Echoing Edward Said, Hochberg suggests an antidote to the current hostility between Jews and Muslims—overcoming historical amnesia. Both Jews and Muslims might recall and condemn their *mutual* degradation at the hands of 19th-century pseudoscience that gave new credence to old-fashioned paranoia about the Semite's "capacity to contaminate, destroy, and undo Europe." As we'll see such apprehension lives on in Replacement

Theory, the métier of white supremacist paranoia in North America and Europe.[54]

The *Protocols*' Afterlife

The *Protocols* emerged from the 19th-century zeitgeist just described. But how significant is the document per se; what of its current impact? As we've seen, it was read and promoted by Henry Ford. His efforts didn't go unnoticed. Hitler's agents gave him a medal—the Grand Cross of the Supreme Order of the German Eagle. And, even now—as Amazon reviews reveal—readers "are awakened" by the *Protocols*' paranoid themes. All that said, we contend the document's impact is overstated: *While the Protocols make Jews the scapegoat for human misery, many writers make the Protocols the scapegoat for the horrors inflicted upon Jews.* Jeremiads abound: In Norman Cohn's words: Not only are the *Protocols* a "Warrant for Genocide," or an "atrocity-producing" tract, they are an "imaginary document that leads to real genocide."[55] Like historian Richard Levy we ask rhetorically: "Would ... [Nazi] actions have been different had there never existed a *Protocols of the Elders of Zion?*"[56] Would the white supremacists who terrorized Charlottesville have stayed home if the *Protocols* had never been forged? This is not to suggest that it's irrelevant. *The Protocols reflect, promote, and legitimize Judeophobia; however, they are a catalyst, an accelerant, not a cause.*

This is not to suggest that *Protocols*' themes and libels faded into obscurity. On the contrary, variations are alive and demented in what we'll call "Protocols 2.0" neoclassic conspiracy theology, and Protocols 3.0, the interactive, mystery game known as QAnon.

Protocols 2.0: The Fatal Attraction of Classical Conspiracy Theology

The classical conspiracy theologies of modernity are not obsolete: Apprehensive about the fragility of their white privilege, mass murderers Timothy McVeigh and Anders Breivik embraced the faith-based dogma, the theology, that drove the narratives in works such as *The Turner Diaries,* and *Eurabia.*[57]

It appears that McVeigh was captivated by a neoclassic variation of the *Protocols, The Turner Diaries.* The infamous novel, found in his car, glorifies bombing federal facilities—a triumphant move in guerilla warfare intended to liberate the nation from government tyranny and the pernicious influence of Jews, immigrants, and other undesirables. Writing for the Center for Analysis of the Radical Right, Kesa White explains:

Before his attacks, McVeigh read "The Turner Diaries," a novel about the violent overthrow of the federal government that eventually leads to a race war. The novel plays a crucial role in solidifying white dominance by glorifying violence ... [a] narrative for a race war.[58]

As the novel opens, Jews are confiscating the patriots' guns, and the "Zionist Occupied Government" is replacing white Europeans with "lesser breeds"—namely Muslims. Courageous resisters strike back and incinerate government buildings. (Could it be that federal attacks on cultists in Ruby Ridge, Idaho, and Waco, Texas, convinced McVeigh that the *Diaries* was a call to arms?) The fictional Earl Turner writes: "Our bomb went off ... the damage is immense. We have certainly disrupted a major portion of the ... FBI's operations."[59] And so, on the second anniversary of the federal attack on the Waco compound, McVeigh turned Pierce's fiction to reality: He detonated the truck bomb that destroyed the Murrah Federal Building in Oklahoma City: 168 civilians (including 19 children) perished.

McVeigh, however, was not the only conspiracy theologian. Motivated by Islamophobic paranoia, certain journalists and law enforcement officials reflexively blamed Arabs and Muslims (the two are usually conflated). Writing in the *Chicago Tribune* as the ruins cooled, syndicated columnist Mike Royko simply couldn't wait to exact revenge by attacking Arabs. He allowed that:

> I would have no objection if we picked out a country that is a likely suspect and bombed some oil fields, refineries, bridges, highways, industrial complexes .... If it happens to be the wrong country, well, too bad, but it's likely it did something to deserve it anyway.[60]

Federal agents sought out individuals who appeared Middle Eastern. Abraham Ahmad, a blameless American citizen of Jordanian origins, was arrested attempting to board a plane. Subsequently, the perpetrator, white supremacist McVeigh, was captured, convicted, and executed for committing the heinous deed. Like the fictional Earl Turner, the real Timothy McVeigh had no remorse. He is lionized on the websites of the postmodern gamers who aspire to better his kill score.

The author, William Pierce, assures the reader that *The Turner Diaries* bears no responsibility for the deed. Never mind that, interviewed prior to McVeigh's execution, he praised McVeigh as a man of principle willing to accept the consequences for what he did. (McVeigh was arrested fleeing the scene.) Subsequent supremacists celebrate McVeigh and preach the gospel of "Replacement Theory."[61] Norwegian supremacist, Anders Breivik idolized McVeigh.

Asne Seierstad's Breivik biography locates the mass murderer in a liminal space betwixt and between classical conspiracy theory and the gamified postmodern conspiracism of the Internet. In her account, like the postmodern conspiracists who celebrate his massacre, he found Internet gamification irresistible: "Breivik became obsessed with the online game *World of Warcraft* which he would sometimes play for 17 straight hours."[62] Breivik, driven by recognition hunger, strived to make a name for himself. Enthralled by neoclassic texts such as *Eurabia*, he sought recognition by thwarting the Muslim invasion of Scandinavia.[63] His "twisted ideology" precipitated the murder of 8 individuals near government buildings, and 69 sons and daughters of Norwegian elites at a summer camp: He accused their parents of race betrayal for admitting Muslim refugees. His 1500-page diatribe raged against liberalism, multiculturalism, and to be sure, Muslims. As journalist J.M. Berger concludes: "The Norwegian extremist Anders Behring Breivik set the bar for what an individual terrorist could accomplish."[64]

Breivik posted his manifesto on *Stormfront*, a neo-Nazi Internet message board. And yet, he didn't demonize all Jews: Commendable Zionists created their own ethno-state and fought Muslims; unfortunately, despicable Jews brought multiculturalism and Muslims to Norway. Like McVeigh, Breivik was enraged by ruling elites who permitted this immigration—the invaders profaned his sacred white spaces. He praised Bat Ye'or's conspiracy theory *Eurabia*[65] and lauded American Islamophobes, such as Richard Spencer, and local Islamophobes for revealing an alleged plot to turn Europe into an appendage of the Arab/Muslim world. However, *Stormfront* maligned Breivik for murdering white Norwegian children, not despised Muslims.

Breivik's Islamophobia was not based upon personal encounters, the prospect of Oslo being governed by Shira Law, or an imminent invasion from principalities of the Greater Middle East. "The Muslim" was a phantasm threatening to forever change Scandinavian demographics and sensibility. Journalist Sindre Bangstad explains Breivik's anticipatory anxiety in "Eurabia Comes to Norway":

> Andres Behring Breivik ... was profoundly inspired by what has become known as the Eurabia genre ... [i.e. Replacement Theory] central to understanding the worldviews of extreme right-wing "counter-jihadists." It is a conspiratorial genre in which a central rhetorical trope is that Europe is on the verge of being taken over by Muslims.[66]

Like traditional conspiracy theorists before him, Breivik strived to appear erudite and authoritative by indulging in pedantic documentation (reminiscent of the padded references larded in many a student term paper). His bibliography references works ranging from Plato through Tolstoy. He even alludes to Kant's *Critique of Pure Reason*, but somehow omits *Perpetual Peace*—the philosopher's proposal for world government. However, classical Islamophobe conspiracy theory held its sway, not the Western canon.

Protocols 3.0: QAnon

QAnon illustrates the unbridled, shameless workings of the pornographic imagination striving for shock and recognition. Only such an imagination could envision Hillary Clinton molesting and killing children and drinking their blood in Satanic rites. Has the conspiracists' pornographic imagination reached the outer limits of the despicable? Does something even more odious lie in wait? At this point all we can do is move in for a closer look at one of the latest ginned-up variations on *Protocol* themes. Mike Rothschild offers considerable insight:

> QAnon: It is far from original. In fact, very little of Q's mythology originates with Q. A rich tapestry of conspiracy theories, ancient hatreds, currency scams, moral panics, and social media rumors were stitched together to make QAnon, but few of these ideas are entirely new, nor is their original provenance difficult to trace.[67]

On October 28, 2017, an anonymous Internet subscriber known as Q posted on 4chan—the go-to website for conspiracists, bigots, and virtually every variety of attention-craving eccentrics. QAnon became a suspenseful, interactive game played in a cybernated Skinner Box: Hooked participants anxiously await the next random reward—a "Q-drop" (mind-blowing secret intelligence from a highly placed insider). Like its ancestral *Protocols*, QAnon's authorship remains clouded in mystery—enhanced suspense. Nevertheless, as Rothschild suggests, its heritage can be traced. He plausibly speculates:

> It's overwhelmingly likely that Q is … an undistinguished 4chan LARP that caught on because it told a story about bad people being punished and good people doing the punishing. Just as Q repurposed parts of countless older scams and tropes, it's inevitable that Q itself will be repurposed by something else.[68]

Q foretold the imminent arrest of Hillary Clinton. The posting was done in what was supposed to be the staccato, abbreviated style of a military intelligence communique: "HRC extradition already in motion … expect massive riots." Q's signature—failed predictions—is invariably rationalized. The cognoscenti know that disinformation is an ingenious ploy intended to deceive those who would foil Q's efforts to bring on The Storm—the apocalypse that would smash the deep state.

Why do people play the Q-game in the first place; what's the attraction? Like Rothschild, we wonder about what gnawing void QAnon fills in the lives of those who embrace it. Recall Our Candidate? A man who dreaded his life would end in lonely despair. We imagine the dejected lad on a lonely shore sealing a message in a bottle, casting it into the sea, and wistfully awaiting response; he implores the void: "Give me a white man a reason to live .... How do you go on living?"[69] Evidently, his white privilege did not provide all he deserved. We wouldn't be surprised if he had a popular bumper sticker on his beat-up pickup truck—"Life's a bitch then you die." Recall: An anonymous respondent urged him to write a book exposing the Jews pedophilia and perversion. It's been done time and again, and besides—who reads? Where can Our Candidate make a name for himself?

We suggested—sardonically to be sure—commenting on white supremacist theology on one of the transgressive websites. Of course, the site is probably dominated by an acclaimed edgelord; he would be reduced to a mere spectator once again. Could his fate lie with QAnon? This latest iteration of the *Protocols*' takes the supremacist's imagination on its farthest magical mystery tour. Hillary is not wicked because she is brainwashed and mind-controlled. She, like the rest of the characters in the Manichean morality play, is intrinsically and irredeemably evil. The interactive game, of course, needs other super villains—who else but the Jews? A search of the archive of QAnon-favored sites, 8chan and 8kun for the word "Jew":

> Brings up well over one hundred thousand[references]. In fact, 8chan has been rated as one of the most anti-Semitic places on the Internet by the Anti-Defamation League, full of targeted harassment against Jewish journalists, praise of anti-Semitic mass shooters, and an endless supply of anti-Jewish memes references.[70]

In addition to blood-drinking ghoul Hillary Clinton, closet Muslim Barak Obama plots evil deeds. Hillary's acolytes spread Satanic villainy; like Dan Brown's heroes we must look for clues: Movies, music, and television are redolent with Satanic symbols—if we know what to look for. These artifacts are maliciously designed to weaken our resolve and critical faculties. The cabal also promotes vaccines, cheap sugary food, and antibiotics on us to ensure we never break the chains of our mental and physical slavery. The Jews, namely George Soros and the Rothschild banking dynasty (again the author mentions no relation), pull the strings. But what would Manichean drama be without a hero? Donald Trump plays a messianic, redeemer role.

Working with Q, the second coming of Trump will bring on The Storm, execute malefactors, and make America *very* great for the first time.

QAnon dramatis personae are novel, contemporary characters. (Old villains such as Henry Kissinger are long retired.) Seeing lackluster Hillary as a blood-curdling witch does require suspending disbelief. However, if QAnon only changed the cast and scenery, it might well become a tiresome rerun of tried and untrue conspiracism—boredom is the death knell of conspiracism. However, QAnon captivates because it introduces the novel and unexpected—*participation*.

The antique *Protocols* merely offered a ringside seat. Q puts us in the action, in the Intel—we get drops (clues). For some, it may simply be make-believe, an enjoyable pastime like being written into a Dan Brown novel. Others, as we've seen, take it seriously, and invade businesses, even the Capitol. Perhaps they believe their courageous action will help bring on the storm. In any case, whoever conjured-up QAnon knew that in a digital world "We are increasingly physically isolated and alone, particularly in the time of COVID-19, this combination of a participatory game played alongside a digital community against an easy scapegoat is hugely compelling."[71]

Notes

1 David Dunlap, *New York Times*, October 27, 2016.
2 The text refers to Gentiles as "goyim."
3 *The Protocols of the Learned Elders of Zion*, trans. Victor E. Marsden (Austin: River Crest Publishing, 2011). [Hereafter referred to as the *Protocols*.]
4 See Jonathan Heil, "Thomas of Monmouth and the Protocols of the Sages of Narbonne," in *The Paranoid Apocalypse: A Hundred-Year Retrospective on The Protocols of the Elders of Zion* (Elie Wiesel Center for Judaic Studies Series), Kindle Edition, ed. Stephen T. Katz (New York: New York University Press, 2011), pp. 56–76. [Hereafter abbreviated PA.]
5 David Baddiel, "Short on a Conspiracy Theory? You Can Always Blame the Jews," *Guardian*, July 22, 2015, accessed October 26, 2021, https://theguardian.com/commentisfree/2015/conspiracy-theory-jews-david-cameron-antisemitism-extremism.
6 See Mike Rothschild's insightful account of QAnon, in *The Storm Is upon Us* (Brooklyn: Melville House, 2021), p. 49. The author hastens to add that he is not related to the Rothschild dynasty—a perennial target of conspiracists.
7 Daniel Torday, "The Incoherence of Hate: Reading the Protocols of the Elders of Zion," *Literary Hub*, accessed October 4, 2021, https://lithub.comm/the-incoherence-of-hate-reading-the-protocols-of-the-elders-of- zion.
8 Texe Marrs, "Foreword: Protocols Proven by the Sweep of History," in *Protocols*, p. 6.
9 Ibid., p. 13.
10 Ford draws these distinctions in *Protocols*, pp. 15–23.
11 Ibid., p. 28.

12 James Rudin, "The Dark Legacy of Henry Ford's Anti-Semitism," *Washington Post*, October 10, 2014, accessed October 6, 2012, https://www.washintonpost .com/national/religion/the-dark-l . . .11e4-877c-335bb53ffe736-story.htm?tid=u sw_passupdateepg.

13 Ibid.

14 Quoted by Torday, "The Incoherence of Hate."

15 Location 2217.

16 Ibid., p. 2407.

17 Ibid., p. 2621.

18 Ibid., p. 2288.

19 Ibid., Locations 2407–2472.

20 Esther Webman (ed.), *The Global Impact of the Protocols of the Elders of Zion: A Century-Old Myth. (Routledge Jewish Studies Series)*, Kindle edition (New York: Routledge, 2011), location 292.

21 Norman Cohn, *Warrant for Genocide: The Myth of the Jewish World-Conspiracy and the Protocols of the Elders of Zion* (London: Serif, 2005), p. 118.

22 Disputing the suspected French origins of *The Protocols*, Cesare G. De Michelis authored *The Non-existent Manuscript: A Study of the Protocols of the Sages of Zion*, Studies in Antisemitism Series (Lincoln: University of Nebraska Press, 2004).

23 Considerable scholarly ink is spilt regarding the controversy. Webman, *The Global Impact of the Protocols of the Elders of Zion*. According to Cohn's controversial account, a Czarist police agent, Pytor Rachkovsky forged the text. Richard S. Levy asks the right question in "Setting the Record Straight Regarding the Protocols of the Elders of Zion: A Fool's Errand?" in *Nexus Two: Essays in German Jewish Studies*, ed. Williams Collins Donahue and Martha B. Heller (Camden: Boydell & Brewer, 2018), pp. 43–61. Amid contesting speculation, the fabrication's origins remain clouded in mystery.

24 Quoted by Webman, *The Global Impact of the Protocols of the Elders of Zion*, Kindle location 6809.

25 Quoted by Cohn, *Warrant for Genocide*, p. 97.

26 Ibid., p. 58.

27 Cohn, *Warrant for Genocide*, p. 101.

28 In addition to the biographical studies of Cohn and Landes and Katz, see excerpts from Nilus' autobiography reproduced by St. John's Russian Orthodox Church in Canberra Australia: accessed August 17, 2019, webmaster@stjohnthebaptist .org.au.

29 See Cohn's discussion, pp. 96–102.

30 Quoted by Kenneth Jacobson, "The Protocols: Myth and History," *Anti-Defamation League*, 1981, accessed, Oct. 21, 2021, https://www.adl.org/sites /default/files/documents/assets/pdf/anti-semitism/united-states/the-protocols -myth-and-history-1981.pdf.

31 See "Protocols of The Elders of Zion: Key Dates" (Washington, DC: United States Holocaust Museum), accessed October 10, 2021, https//encyclopedia .ushmm.org./content/en/article/protoc))ols-of-the-elders-of-zion.

32 Maurice Joly, *Dialogue between Montesquieu and Machiavelli in Hell*, trans. John Waggoner (Lanham: Lexington Books, 2002).

33 Philip P. Graves, "The Truth about 'The Protocols': A Literary Forgery: From the *Times* of August 16, 17 and 18, 1921," *London Times*, 1921, accessed October 16, 2021, https://www.worldcat.org/title/truth-about-the-protocols-a

-literary-forgery-from-the-times-of-august-16-17-and-18-1921/oclc/836129786
?referer=di&ht=edition. Graves' research revealed plagiarism and paraphrasing
from Maurice Joly's *Enfers entre Montesquieu et Marchievel*, (*Dialogue
between Montesquieu and Machiavelli in Hell*). Norman Cohn reveals the role
of Hermann Goedsche's Biarritz in fabricating the *Protocols.*

34 *The London Times* printed details about Graves' investigation in a brochure
    entitled *The Truth About the Protocols—A Literary Forgery*, accessed October
    29, 2021.

35 Cohn, *Warrant for Genocide*, pp. 38–41.

36 Richard Landes, "Jewish Self-Criticism, Progressive Moral Schadenfruede, and
    the Suicide of Reason: Reflections on the Protocols in the 'Postmodern' era",
    *The Paranoid Apocalypse: A Hundred-Year Retrospective on the Protocols of
    the Elders of Zion*, ed. Richard Landes and Steven T. Katz (New York: New
    York University Press, 2012), Location 510.

37 Ibid.

38 Ibid., Locations 567–575.

39 See Stephen B. Smith's Preface in his *Modernity and Its Discontents* (New
    Haven and London: Yale University Press, 2006). Smith allows that Freud's title,
    "Civilization and Its Discontents," inspired his title. Freud's work is relevant
    here: We pay a high price for civilized modernity: when can't do what we'd
    passionately love to do—act out our erotic and destructive urges. No wonder
    Mick Jagger laments, "I can't get no satisfaction."

40 E.A. Burtt, *The Metaphysical Foundations of Modern Science* (Mineola, NY:
    Dover, 2003), p. 303.

41 Joseph Bottum, "Why Catholics Need Not Choose Between Science and
    Wonder," *New Atlantis*, Summer 2013, p. 3, accessed October 29, 2021, https://
    www.thenewatlantis.com/publications/disenchantment-and-its-discontents.

42 Michael Goldfarb, *Emancipation: How Liberating Europe's Jews from the
    Ghetto Led to Revolution and Renaissance*, Kindle Edition (New York: Simon
    & Schuster, 2009), Location 58.

43 Ibid., p. 62.

44 Quoted in "88 Famous Quotes from Disraeli," in *Quotes the Famous People.com.*

45 Adam Gopnik, "Trial of the Century," *New Yorker*, September 28, 2009,
    accessed October 3, 2021, https://www.newyorker.com/magazine/2009/09/28/
    trial-of-the-century.

46 Reza Zia-Ebrahimi, "There is No Islamophobic Elephant in This Room-- A
    reflection on Houellebecq's Submission and its Reception," *ReOrient The
    Journal of Critical Muslim Studies -Blog,* May 1, 2007, accessed November
    3, 2021, https://www.criticalmuslimstudies.co.uk/there-is-no-islamophobic-ele-
    phant-in-this-room-a-reflection-on-houellebecqs-submission-and-its-reception/.

47 The Hebrew University's *Moshe Zimmerman*, aptly entitles his study *Wilhelm
    Marr: The Patriarch of Anti-Semitism* (New York: Oxford University Press, 1986).

48 Wilhelm Marr, "The Victory of Judaism over Germandom," cited in *German
    History in Document and Images*, accessed November 1, 2021, germanhistory-
    docs.ghi-dc.org/.

49 Binjamin W. Segel, "Preface," *A Lie and a Libel*. ed. R. S. Levy (Lincoln:
    University of Nebraska Press, (1995), p. x.

50 Hochberg, analyzes the p. 206.

51 Quoted by Gil Z. Hochberg, "'Remembering Semitism' or 'on the Prospect of
    Re-Membering the Semites'," *ReOrient* 1, no. 2 (2016), p. 203.

52 Hochberg, p. 203.

53 Ibid., p. 217.

54 Ibid., p. 213.

55 As we've seen, Norman Cohn entitled his influential study, *Warrant for Genocide: The Myth of the Jewish World-Conspiracy and the Protocols of the Elders of Zion.*

56 Richard S. Levy, *A Lie and A Libel: The History of the Protocols of the Elders of Zion* (Lincoln: University of Nebraska Press, 1996), pp. 31–32.

57 The classical theory is of course *The Protocols.* Neoclassical derivatives include William Pierce, *The Turner Diaries* (Mountain City, Tennessee: Cosmotheist Books, 2019), The book is popular, in its sixth printing. See Bat Ye'or (pseudonym of Gisele Littman) *Eurabia: The Euro-Arab Axis* (Vancouver: Fairleigh Dickinson University Press, 2005); a Muslim doppelganger of *Protocol* themes—analyzed in in Chapter 3. The postmodern Internet is replete with memes derived from Protocol slanders against Jews—discussed in Chapter 4.

58 Kesa White, "Why the Oklahoma City Bombing Continues to Cast A Shadow Over America," *Radio Free*, August 12, 2021, accessed August 14, 2021, https://www.radiofree.org/2021/08/12/why-the-oklahoma-bombing-continues-to-cast-a-shadow-over-america/.

59 *The Turner Diaries*, p. 38.

60 See "Oklahoma City Bombing When Arabs Were Blamed," *Chicago Tribune,* April 9, 1995, accessed July 11, 2021, https://www.siasat.com/oklahoma-bombing-when-arabs-were-blamed-homegrown-attack-1876918/. Federal agents singled out individuals of Middle Eastern appearance. One can only wonder about the transgressions, in Royko's view, committed by the civilians who would perish.

61 See Renaud Camus, *The Great Replacement* (Paris: Chez l'auteur, November 10, 2018).

62 See Dwight Garner, "Review: 'One of Us,' by Asne Seierstad on Anders Breivik's Rampage in Norway," *New York Times*, April 9, 2015.

63 Old-fashioned vile graffiti has evolved into Internet memes. The "shitposter" acclaimed for the most transgressive memes becomes the exalted "edgelord."

64 J.M. Berger, "The Dangerous Spread of Extremist Manifestos: By Sharing the Writings of Terrorists, Media Outlets Can Amplify Their Impact," *The Atlantic*, February 26, 2019. Ironically, is Berger spreading the impact, are we?

65 See Bat Ye'or (pseudonym of Gisele Littman) *Eurabia: The Euro-Arab Axis* (Vancouver: Fairleigh Dickinson University Press, 2005); this work will be analyzed in detail in Chapter 3. Bat Ye'or's jeremiad is yet to materialize; we are not aware of Europeans living under Sharia Law.

66 Sindre Bangstad, "Eurabia Comes to Norway," *Sosialantropologisk Institutt (SAI)*, June 19, 2013, accessed August 14, 2021, https://www.sv.uio.no/sai/forskning/publikasjoner/artikler/2013/eurabia-comes-to-norway.html.

67 Rothschild, *The Storm is Upon Us*, p. 49.

68 Ibid., p. 240; LARP, it may be recalled, is an acronym for "life action role playing." Bringing video games to life, many might recall the Pokemon-Go craze when mostly young people, fixated on cell phones, wandered about looking for clues. Could it be that, as we write, some of these individuals are fixated once again unraveling QAnon "drops"—enigmatic clues about the coming storm? As we'll see in Chapter 4, those who terrorize our mosques and synagogues pretend they are crusaders, medieval knights, or heroic soldiers "going in" on a sacred mission.

69 Ava Kofman, Moira Weigel, and Francis Tseng, "White Supremacy's Gateway to The American Mind," *The Atlantic*, April 7, 2020, accessed October 11, 2021.

70 See "Full Transcription of the Original Posts from Q on 4chan & 8chan.," accessed December 15, 2021, krypt3ia.files.wordpress.com/2018/08/q_s_posts_-_cbts_-_7-2-0.pdf.

71 Ibid., p. 11.

3 The Muslim Brotherhood(s)

If Frank Gaffney Jr. had his way, average hard-working Americans of the Muslim faith would be dragged before Congress to face such questions as, "Are you now, or have you ever been, a member of the Muslim Brotherhood?"[1]

Gaffney's way did come to pass immediately after 9/11 as thousands of innocent Arabs and Muslims were dragged into courts and jails, surveilled, and asked about their religious proclivities. The magical Arab of Disney cartoons is no more: Technicolor images of magic carpets wafting amid bejeweled palaces are gone. Post-9/11, the Arab (conflated with the Muslim) shape-shifts from magician to monster. The Arab is the boogeyman who came to us in febrile, childhood nightmares.[2] In the conspiracist imagination, like the perfidious Jew, the Arab conspires to destroy all that is sacred—white genocide.

One of the initial contemporary fantasies of a worldwide Muslim conspiracy is promoted in *Eurabia* theory: The claim that Muslims are trying to take control of Europe through concerted efforts by forging alliances with liberal European political leaders and multiculturalists. They seek to undermine European culture, overwhelm its cities with foreigners, and subjugate its people to Sharia law.

The Brothers operate primarily in the Greater Middle East, not on the plains of Oklahoma. They have neither the intention nor the ability to influence American domestic and foreign policy. Opposing the conspiracists' simple-minded view, we show that the Muslim Brotherhood is not a unitary seamless organization, let alone a singular conspiracy bent on establishing a planetary caliphate. To reiterate: *The Brotherhoods* are loosely organized, contesting affiliates. Contrary to conspiracist caricatures, The Brotherhoods cover the political spectrum from archconservative to social democrat.[3]

Ruminations about the Muslim Brotherhoods (MB) amplify this threat and bring it to American shores. The organization which began in Egypt long

DOI: 10.4324/9781003207894-3

ago supposedly conspires to subvert Western democratic systems, thereby reducing its peoples to the status of *Dhimmis*, a minority group living under Muslim rule. Curiously, the Muslim Brothers are portrayed, in Bat Ye'or's (pseudonym) book, *Eurabia: The Euro-Arab Axis*,[4] as co-conspirators with Arab regimes determined to undermine European civilization: a particularly bizarre assertion in light of the tumultuous, often violent history between secular Arab regimes and the MB. Such facts, of course, are ignored by those who live in the conspiratorial imagination—it would negate the faulty premise upon which these conspiracies rest. (As previously suggested, the conspiracy theories of modernity ignore cognitive dissonance.)

To reiterate, the MB is erroneously referred to as a unitary organization; however, its affiliates embody diverse, even contesting, ideologies and practices—not unlike the far-ranging variety of Protestant denominations. Initiated by a school teacher Hassan Al Banna in Egypt (in 1928) as a call for renewed faith, it quickly spread to several countries in the Middle East.[5] The idea was simple: Muslims should have a voice in their own governance (remember, the Middle East was steeped in Marxist, Socialist, secularist, and Nationalist parties at the time). These ideologies were rightly seen as foreign: alien ideologies adopted from the colonizers incompatible with the mores of Muslim-majority nations. Ironically, the only ideology forbidden in the government sphere was a faith to which most citizens subscribed— namely Islam.

Contrary to conspiracist fantasies, the Muslim world is far from a unified, coherent whole. Not surprisingly the ideology of the original Brotherhood became fragmented: Hardliners wanted to live under self-imposed Sharia (Islamic Law), while others simply envisioned self-representation in a pluralistic Middle East.[6] Indeed, many Muslim fundamentalists (e.g., Salafis and Wahabbis) saw competing Brotherhoods as too political—too leftist for their orthodox vision of Islamic governance. According to an *Al-Jazeera* report, the MB's ideology is predominantly focused on reforming the current political structures of the Arab world, the report states that the MB embraces:

> political activism and social responsibility, organizing charitable works and social support programmes as part of its outreach to its core support base of lower-income populations ... The members of the MB represent a broad spectrum of interpretations of the initial ideology ... embrac[ing] a more pragmatic idea...urging political participation and cooperation.[7]

Conspiracists, fantasizing about collusion between Arab States and the Brothers, don't realize (or acknowledge) that many Arab States fight to subdue—even annihilate—the MB: They perceive the group as a threat to *their* survival. (Amin's father, falsely accused of Brotherhood membership, spent time in a Syrian prison.) *We can't help but wonder who ultimately benefits from the continued existence of puppet regimes in the Middle East.* Currently, Qatar and Turkey are the only Muslim-majority nations that do not designate the MB a terrorist organization. This information—an overlooked, inconvenient truth to put it charitably—calls into question Bat Ye'or's thesis. Arab regimes don't collude with the Brotherhood to conquer Europe; on the contrary, they're too busy persecuting the organization. Conspiracists, seldom overly concerned with facts, ignore the historical and continued animosity between those secular regimes and the MB.

Egypt's recent history adds to the voluminous body of evidence against Bat Ye'or's thesis, conveniently ignored by conspirarists. Consider Abdel Fattah Al-Sisi's coup d'etat in 2013 against then-president Mohamed Morsi, a democratically elected president with ties to the MB. Morsi was sentenced to 25 years in prison (with hard labor) and later sentenced to death for his alleged collaboration with extremist groups.

Notable Islamophobes

We turn to the vivid imaginations of conspiracists such as Frank Gaffney, Jr., Richard Spencer, and Pam Geller: Their alarmism—verging on panic—is bereft of documented, compelling evidence. For Gaffney, a man who once railed against the Red Scare, and the eventual takeover of America by Soviet Communists:[8] The old prophecies failed—a rather telling refutation of his widely shared conspiracy theory. However, 9/11 provided fertile ground, to understate the case, for new conspiracy theories along with a new Internet venue for postmodern conspiracism. Gaffney (*who advised President Trump*) exposed yet another mortal, conspiratorial threat—this time the Muslim Brotherhood. As we'll see, his ruminations relied primarily upon innuendo and guilt by association. His long-ago jeremiads never came to pass. Nevertheless, the faithful still await the dreaded day.

Quite obviously, Gaffney has little in common with Nilus, an alarmist of yesteryear who breathlessly promoted the *Protocols*, but could it be that the cunning of history entrapped both in a dialectic interplay of despair and fanaticism? Consider Gaffney's despair. The Soviet Union imploded during the Reagan Administration as did Gaffney's anti-communist life project; his career stalled. As we've suggested, those who become deeply involved in a failed project fall into a nihilistic chasm devoid of meaning. They fill the chasm with passionate devotion to yet another heroic project. For Gaffney, the Soviet communists didn't have the decency to vindicate his warnings—the regime collapsed without fulfilling his prophecies.

Just as Nilus suffered career setbacks, Gaffney's darkest moment came in 1987. After working for President Ronald Reagan, he was named acting assistant secretary of defense, but the Senate did not confirm his nomination.[9] Shortly thereafter, Gaffney founded the Center for Security Policy (a think tank that initially was nothing more than Gaffney, his computer, a printer, and a fax machine) dedicated to protecting America from all who would destroy it. Initially, Gaffney's new project didn't gain traction. 9/11 changed everything: Apocalyptic conspiracism became a new passion—terrorist cells were somehow metastasizing throughout the land. Multicolored terrorism alerts became commonplace.

Popularizing Freud's *Group Psychology*, Eric Hoffer argues that the true believer loses him/herself in an idea and yearns to lose the self in the collective whole.[10] For Hoffer, the biblical figure Saul was no different than Paul, both were zealots. Perhaps the same can be said for a fervent anti-communist who becomes a latter-day Islamophobe. Fortunately, most conspiracists don't resort to violence. Unfortunately, some do. (We confront this issue in Chapter 4.) Like the *Protocols*, "The Project" is the proverbial "smoking gun" providing undeniable evidence of a conspiracy for those with a will to believe.

The Project

The *Protocols* live on in a doppelganger—"The Project." The English translation, provided by the Bridge Initiative at Georgetown University, is nothing short of embarrassing to read—the Arabic version isn't any better. The document purportedly highlights the MB's plan for global domination through the use of vague, often incoherent bullet points. Broken down, the document is formatted in the following way: *points of departure*, followed by *elements, procedures, and suggested missions*. Such a format gives the document an aura of scholarly rigor and meticulous planning; the substance suggests otherwise. By way of example: "The establishment of an Islamic State ... aimed at gaining control of local power";[11] and another "to conduct a modern study on the concept of support for the dawa [proselytization] ... on the men of influence in the State and the country,"[12] and yet another "to use ... surveillance ... to gather information and adopt a ... warning system serving the worldwide Islamic movement."[13] Throughout the document, the authors rely on generalities, broad points intended to convey a singular message—eventual global domination. Curiously, the main points advance a general fear of what's to come, but conspicuously absent are the technical strategies required to get there—could it be that the authors intend to promote paranoia, not instructions? Public administrators who engage in strategic planning know that grand goals should be preceded by detailed strategies and properly aligned and meticulously planned steps: Quite possibly the authors never worked for an organization that developed strategic plans—perhaps they simply imitated the Protocols.

The mirror imaging intrigues: The strategies for domination put forth in the document are actually those carried out by the West against Muslims. Consider the point about the use of mass surveillance and the adoption of an effective warning system. The reader may recall that from 2001 to 2014, the New York City Police Department (NYPD) under the leadership of Mayor Michael Bloomberg engaged in the Muslim Surveillance and Mapping Program. This secret program relied on the Demographics Unit which sent agents to spy on mosques, student groups, businesses, and areas of the city frequented by Arab and Muslim citizens to gather information on 28 "ancestries of interest."[14] Details surrounding this covert program remained elusive for years and brought to light after extensive investigative journalism exposed the illegal cooperation between the NYPD and CIA—an actual conspiracy since the CIA is not permitted to function domestically. While this program was made in America, it is not unique to the United States; other Western nations have instituted similarly controversial legislation.[15]

Ominously, the *Project*'s encouragement to deploy an early warning system sounds eerily similar to that employed by George W. Bush's administration following the 9/11 attacks, and later adopted by the Department of Homeland Security (DHS) after its creation in 2003.[16] Readers may recall the color-coded system employed by the DHS and its international counterparts at airports and television monitors following incidents deemed to be acts of international terrorism; of course who knew what the colors meant? Even government officials were clueless when asked.

Could the *Project* be mere chicanery? Given the telling similarities, it is appropriate to ask: Was this *Protocols* doppelganger contrived by Machiavellian actors hoping to prey upon the naivete of the unsophisticated by creating phantoms?

Much like the *Protocols*, we locate the *Project* in modernity. While the document is obviously false, the authors nonetheless point to actual possibilities, thus lending credence to their work. For example, it is quite feasible for a group to influence educational systems: consider required studies of the Holocaust or opposition to slavery, the civil rights, and women's suffrage movements in the United States. Such attempts to enrich the educational curriculum are not uniquely American; they're found in many countries with strained race relations or multicultural histories. In Australia for instance, the dedicated work of activists and educators resulted in the inclusion of topics such as Aboriginal and Torres Strait Islander histories and cultures within the educational curriculum.[17]

Eurabia

A favorite among contemporary mass shooters and conspiracists, Bat Ye'or's (Pseudonym) *Eurabia: The Euro-Arab Axis* is cited frequently as evidence of the inevitable takeover and domination of Western civilization in screeds and posted manifestos—the author (whose real name is Gisele Littman), is herself an Egyptian-born Jewish woman. This widely cited claim that the Muslim Brotherhood is colluding with Arab regimes to undermine European and Western governments is not without its glaring inconsistencies, fallacies, and imagery eerily similar to the *Protocols*. Consider the description found on Amazon's book page which tells us that the book is about:

> The transformation of Europe into "Eurabia," a cultural and political appendage of the Arab/Muslim world. Eurabia is fundamentally anti-Christian, anti-Western, anti-American, and antisemitic. The institution that has been responsible for this transformation … is the Euro-Arab Dialogue, developed by European and Arab politicians and intellectuals over the past thirty years.[18]

The term "appendage" evokes the image of the octopus emblazoned on copies of the *Protocols* and other anti-Jewish literature. This is ironic when one considers that the author of "Eurabia" is Jewish, and cites among her concerns the potential rise of Islamic antisemitism—the similarity is uncanny. Another overlooked irony is the use of this book by white supremacists given the author's apparent concern for increasing antisemitic threats posed by rising Muslim influence. White supremacists rarely have laudatory comments of Jews in their manifestos, and according to most recent polling, Jews remain the single highest targeted group by white supremacist and conservative extremist groups.[19] Could it be that the same white supremacists who rely on this work are also ones who dabble in literature that disparages Jews, such as the *Protocols of the Elders of Zion*? (Most conspiracists embrace several theories.)

We view Bat Ye'or's *Eurabia: The Euro-Arab Axis* as commentary, not the doppelganger of the *Project*. In it, Bat Ye'or ignores what is patently obvious to many, the glaring inconsistencies alluded to earlier. This is not new of course, like her readers, Bat Ye'or is driven by one of several impulses that drive conspiracism—namely a cognitive desire to fill in the void even at the expense of obvious logical fallacies. Two recent studies attempt to investigate the cognitive mechanisms that drive conspiratorial thinking. The authors tell us that meaning-making is a fundamental characteristic of thinking minds. Expose a person to a set of completely unrelated events and observe the complex ways in which human minds create connections, tell stories, and go beyond what is given to imbue chaos with order.[20]

At times, the conspiracist ignores the connections that exist in lieu of an explanation more suitable to his/her narrative—something Bat Ye'or seems to engage in expertly.

Bat Ye'or's overarching concern is the supposed plot by Arab and European leaders to increase the MB's influence throughout Europe. Putting it charitably, her analysis makes dubious, and at times historically inaccurate claims, to argue her premise. The reader need not go too far before spotting some of these ratiocinations. In the first paragraph of the abstract, she asserts that "for over a millennium, *jihad* has been a potent political force that has subjugated and, in some cases, extinguished once powerful centers of Judeo-Christian, Hindu, Buddhist, and other civilizations in Asia, Africa, and Europe."[21]

We encounter a semantic problem here; the term "Judeo-Christian" is rather contemporary, appearing in the mid-20th century. It was weaponized: used to unite Americans against a common set of external enemies (e.g., Communism, Nazism), rather than to create a more tolerant and inclusive society.[22] Bat Ye'or also neglects the historical realities of Christian Europe's mistreatment of Jews—indeed, the very spring from which the well of Judeophobia arises is European Christendom, but this fact gets in the way of her intention: conflating Jewish and Christian identities with European ones while excluding the Islamic one as foreign. As she avers: "This book describes Europe's evolution from a Judeo-Christian civilization, with important post-Enlightenment secular elements, into a post Judeo-Christian civilization that is subservient to the ideology of *jihad* and the Islamic powers that propagate it."[23] The assertion is bereft of evidence. Another deceptive technique conflates Middle East (Arabs) with Islam. She continues by ascribing to Muslims an essence—what she calls the jihad trait. This is an indelible feature that permeates Muslim psyche. Such racializing is eerily similar to what Hitler and the 19th-century philosophers successfully did to Jewish identity; when Jewishness is a race, one can never escape it. Such essentialization is also dismissive of the clear heterogeneity that exists among the world's nearly 1.8 billion Muslims. She states: "the entire Muslim world as we know it today is a product of this 1,300 year-old *jihad* dynamic."[24] She sees no difference in the level, type, or intensity of religious belief among various members who subscribe to Muslim doctrine—news to anyone involved in the endless internecine arguments. Somehow, she overlooks the equally disputatious Christians, Jews, and Buddhists? It is difficult to take her seriously when she tendentiously ignores the obvious.

Lastly, the benefit of hindsight allows us to critique Bat Ye'or's claims about the impending fate of Europe and America's Islamization. Her book was published in 2005, 16 years ago as of this writing. Today, we find Europe and the United States engulfed in right-wing political movements sharing a common theme, burgeoning xenophobia, hate-filled political rhetoric, Islamophobia, Judeophobia, and hate crimes. She wasn't motivated to protect Jews as she claimed. Her agenda involves promoting Zionism which—unlike many progressive Jews—she conflated with Judaism. Indeed, this tactic aims at silencing opponents of Israeli policies, and likening criticism of Israel to antisemitism. She tells us, "I do not believe that Judeophobia and anti-Zionism are common among the majority of Europeans. These attitudes, instead are imposed *nolens volens* on an often-reluctant public by political, media, and religious elites ..."[25] She implies that the political process, popular media, and religious spheres of Europe are subservient to a shadowy force dominating and controlling them—a familiar libel almost out of the pages of the *Protocols*.

Today, Muslims find themselves at the crosshairs of gratuitous, European legislation aimed at their marginalization despite the fact that Bat Ye'or's jeremiads never came to pass. On the contrary, Europe does not bend to Sharia law. Indeed, French officials propose to curb "Islamic separatism"; President Macron claims that "separatism creates the conditions for Islamic radicalism"—a deeply problematic proposition that fails to historicize and contextualize the blight and social conditions that many Muslims endure in supposedly enlightened France. What's left unsaid: France has a long and sordid history of colonization, followed by migration and subsequent ghettoization and radicalization. (Fanon wasn't indicting Swedes when he wrote *The Wretched of the Earth*.)

Macron continues, as if channeling Bat Ye'or: "Islamist separatism is a conscious political-religious project to slowly create a separate parallel and counter-society by repeatedly rejecting French laws, principles and values."[26] Ironically, responding to this concern, he should *increase* the very isolation he condemns? Perhaps the solution does not rest in paradox. Indeed, such a proposal will likely alienate an already marginalized, immiserated group even further. Such a proposal would likely provoke unrest. Of course, Muslim hostility would be attributed to other causes. Governing elites rarely find flaws with their policies and actions. They default to assigning blame, character flaws, real or imagined to the group. American elites also have default positions—common refrains: "These Blacks or Hispanics just like to live in ghettos—they're lazy." Introspection and self-criticism are not elites' strongest suits: Elites and their intellectual enablers don't dwell upon critiques of redlining and other historically racist policies that led to unequal housing development in American towns and cities.

Muslims find themselves in Europe and the United States combatting a growing militant right-wing *white supremacist* threat, as well as coping with institutionalized multifaceted Islamophobia. By way of example, like too many others Bat Ye'or ignores what they promote: the use of Countering Violent Extremism (CVE) policing. CVE policing developed after 9/11 and specifically targets Muslim communities. These policing strategies are in use in many nations around the world, widely applied in the United States and Europe. The essence of such strategies solicits the assistance of citizens in reporting what they deem "suspicious" or "extreme" ideologies. Often, school teachers, members of the clergy, as well as average citizens are recruited into these programs as the eyes and ears of the state. Such policies rely heavily on detecting extreme ideologies, not concrete acts—a chilling effect on free speech for targeted communities. Moreover, these policies widen the social gap between members of marginalized groups and the resources needed for successful integration and social acceptance, by police, teachers, and counselors.[27]

Consider a telling instance of misplaced fears and stereotyping: the infamous Ahmed Mohamed clock incident.[28] Europe and America have become increasingly difficult places for Muslims to feel welcome, let alone dominate, since the publication of Bat Ye'or's book, and the harm that befell fellow Jews at the hand of white supremacists who cite her work should be cause for contrition.

The Muslims Are Coming, while Europe Slept, and the Boogeyman

Islamophobia is not solely a product of conservative, right-wing ideology. We find evidence of Islamophobic tropes emanating from left-wing news agencies and academic centers and self-professed liberals at all levels of society. Edward Said's influential work *Orientalism*[29] can be credited with exposing the myriad of ways that Western scholarship has viewed the Greater Near East, with a gaze of suspicion, disdain, pity, wonder, fear, and loathing. This view of Arabs and Muslims informed scholarship, literature, the arts, and our political understanding of the region, a variegated territory, composed of 17 countries and varied ideologies and sensibilities.

Islamophobia traffics in anticipatory anxiety, and while the apprehension stems from many factors, it is often a phobia premised on the faulty notion that Muslims possess a monopoly on extremism. Efforts to understand Islamophobia often focus heavily on the narrative depicted by right-wing actors, whose disdain for and animus toward Muslims is painfully apparent.

But little attention has been paid to the ways in which Islamophobia is constructed by liberals at all levels of society, from the halls of the academy to major news outlets.

In an attempt to understand and decipher causes of extremism, analysts resort to perceptual shorthand, and several works illuminate this subtle distinction, but none so well as Arun Kundani's *The Muslims Are Coming! Islamophobia, Extremism, and the Domestic War on Terror.*[30] According to Kundani, experts and analysts attempt to understand "Islamic extremism" in one of the following two ways. The first refers to as "culturalism," i.e., "Islamic culture is inherently antithetical to modern, secular containment. It aspires to impose itself on a society against the will of the polity. Further, because the teachings of Islam fail to separate it from the political sphere, the atavisms of religious fanaticism are dangerously introduced into the public realm." Such an understanding, according to Kundani, makes it impossible for the adherent to separate Islam's violent proclivities from itself—they are indelible features of the faith.

Yet another approach to understanding "Islamic extremism" is through what Kundani refers to as "reformism:"

> [Here] rather than the legacy of a premodern, Oriental religion, extremism is the result of twentieth-century ideologues who transformed Islam's essentially benign teachings into an anti-modern, totalitarian, political ideology.

In this view, the classical religious texts themselves are not the basis for terrorism but require the active interpretation of nefarious actors, turning otherwise benign texts into malicious ones. A common thread between culturalists and reformists is that they both manifest Islamophobic tendencies. Indeed, central to both arguments is an ideology "rooted in an alien culture" and thus adhering to the principles put forth by Said's *Orientalism*. Moreover, placing both on a spectrum, we find that culturalists exist on the conservative end of the Islamophobic rhetorical spectrum, suggesting that there is an indelible marker of violence located within Islam that cannot be mitigated without absolute annihilation.

This essentializing feature of the culturalist paradigm features heavily in the ideas of contemporary Islamophobes such as Frank Gaffney Jr., Pamela Geller, as well as authors who peddle conspiracy theories such as Bat Ye'or. On the other end, we find the liberal reformist who contends that Islam's issues are temporal, and merely bringing it into the modern era, and civilizing its people will surely solve its problem. Liberal pundits, activists, and academics were quick to assert their support for the invasion of Iraq in 2003 *if* it meant liberating its women from Islam's repressive grip.

In the end, proponents of both views often justify similar Machiavellian projects—endless wars in the Greater Middle East and beyond to destroy *or* civilize the Muslim "other."

How one defines Islamophobia is self-confessional: How could it not be related to the socially constructed and accepted frames that permeate one's environment? But one does not merely interpret definitions in a linear fashion, accepting dominant narratives as they are without an interplay between the public and the private. Our ideas about the world come to be as a result of a dialectic process known as symbolic interactionism. With regard to Islamophobia, we do not often come to our conclusions through personal experience: Indeed, as with much of what we claim to "know," we rely on sources deemed legitimate such as the trusted media or admired public figures. It is in this way that Khaled Beydoun refines our understanding of what he refers to public and private Islamophobias.[31]

What makes shooters like Tarrant, Bowers, and Earnest revile Muslims and Jews as to deem them fit for annihilation? This question is especially curious when we learn that their encounters with Muslims and Jews were merely vicarious. We would expect the shooters to harbor animus toward these groups if they were once bullied as children by them. Perhaps an altercation at work or a road rage incident may provide sufficient (albeit unreasonable) cause to seek revenge—not so. The shooters never met Muslims or Jews in any deliberate way, or a way that evokes such memories of hatred that they deemed fit to write about in their manifestos. So, we are left asking the question of how private Islamophobia or Judeophobia are inflamed, absent the requisite negative interaction with members of the reviled group? Beydoun's analysis of the intricate interplay between the public and private Islamophobia provides a good launchpad.

The influence of public policy on civic discourse and behavior cannot be ignored. While policy initiatives may seem to the average citizen as distant, often inconsequential debates about issues unrelated to their lives, the reality couldn't be further from the truth—it depends on how we view the policy discourse. Often through mainstream media, the government's official position on a particular group is made public through official declarations or subtle statements. While it may be true that a local town hall meeting to discuss recent policy changes to building codes may be dull, it nonetheless has immediate consequences for residents—far removed as they may seem. Let us consider two opposite yet contemporary examples of the influence of public policy on personal attitudes of citizens toward members of other groups—namely, Cuban refugees in the 1960s and Arab Americans after the September 11 attacks.

Between 1960 and 1962, Presidents Dwight Eisenhower and John F. Kennedy respectively recognized the plight of Cuban refugees fleeing the

Castro regime in Cuba and set out to establish legislation that would expand social services provided to them. This legislation, signed in 1962 under President Kennedy was called the "Migration and Refugee Assistance Act" otherwise known as the Cuban Refugee Program and was intended to provide, among other things, child welfare services and medical care to recently arrived Cuban refugees in Miami.[32] We do not overlook the ulterior political motives of American politicians concerning the Castro regime; however, with regard to the framing of Cuban refugees as neighbors and friends of the American people, worthy of support, compassion, and the expenditure of resources, the effect was positive. President Kennedy's directive to his Secretary of Health, Education, and Welfare, Mr. Abraham Ribicoff, "I want you to make concrete my concern and sympathy for those who have been forced from their homes in Cuba."[33]

It helped that popular culture set the stage in earlier years by depicting an industrious and lovable Cuban immigrant "Ricky Ricardo" on the widely watched sitcom *I Love Lucy*. Cuban American refugees (and their direct descendants) fared well because they were received positively by the government, and such reception was conveyed to the average citizen through explicit and implicit means, resulting in upward assimilation patterns into the American middle class.[34]

Arabs, and by extension Muslims, were not always well represented in American popular culture. As Jack Sheehan's *Reel Bad Arabs: How Hollywood Vilifies a People*[35] revealed, Hollywood depictions of Arabs represented a spectrum of portrayals, from the hypersexual Arab male figure, to the repressed docile female subject, to the depraved lunatic, irrational, and maniacal terrorist who is motivated by an innate and indelible drive to destroy anything progressive, often associated with Western sensibilities. Such depictions set the stage in the American mind for what's to come, depictions of Arabs as magical beings from far away are nonetheless a signal to the average American that "these individuals are not like us." The magical Arab of orientalism is transformed post 9/11 into a monster. Suddenly, the public discourse shifted, and discourse on a formally vague neighbor became solidified in the American psyche—beware of the Arab/Muslim (or anyone appearing as such), for they are the people responsible for the unspeakable violence brought home on our shores.

The signaling was clear and prolonged. Media organizations played back the footage of the collapse of the twin towers and the smoke billowing from the pentagon on an endless loop, all the while images of Arab hijackers scrolled on our television sets around the globe. Arab names became commonly associated with terrorists, and terms like "Jihad" (holy struggle) "madrasa" (religious school) and "hawala" (money transfer) became fodder for self-proclaimed terrorism experts who appeared seemingly overnight to speak on matters unheard of by most Americans. The United States, joined by an international coalition of militaries, went to war mostly in Muslim-majority countries on a mission to root out terrorism. As a proximate cause of the war on terror, security and technology industries cropped up and flourished with innovations meant to keep citizens in America and around the globe secure—from airport scanners to safe rooms, the message to average citizens was clear the boogeyman is out and we're here to keep you safe. We will return to our analysis of the boogeyman analogy later—it suffices to demonstrate that public representation, and the declaration that Arabs should be seen as a threat does have a significant role in signaling to the average American whom they should revile. We call this high fashion hatred.

The interplay between public messaging and private phobias and prejudice is well documented in American social life. Americans look to their government and media organizations for the latest in high fashion hatred—who's the latest group to resent? A few historical examples make this point clear: At the onset of the 20th century, a Protestant led movement against Catholics ushered in the prohibition. Not long after that, Japanese Americans were rounded up and interned in mass concentration camps for no reason other than their race—they didn't pick the right parents! In the 1970s and 1980s, African Americans and Hispanics underwent what became known as a campaign of mass incarceration through the now-failed conservative strategy of post Jim Crow racial exclusion known as the war on drugs. Lastly, the war on terror targets Arabs and Muslims, and those deemed as such through a myriad of security initiatives and the rise of the surveillance state. These historical accounts share the following connections between the public and the private: The media and criminal justice systems become important tools in reinforcing the image of the despised group. Members of the group are at once cast as the "other" and thus thrust into the tentacles of the criminal justice system, a system designed to control those elements deemed unfit for American sensibilities. In turn, the media uses images of these individuals captured by the criminal justice system to reinforce their inferior social status.

As we have seen, the shooters were moved by signals emanating from the highest places. Their hate was guided by a social construction, a perfect storm of mass hysteria and paranoia, a deliberate and sustained media campaign, as well as questionable public policies and declarations aimed not at resolving deeply complex social problems, but at scapegoating certain groups and scoring political points at the expense of socially and politically marginal members of society. The shooters were thus responding to what they believed was a duty incumbent upon them—to return to normal that which the boogeyman had come to strip away. The boogeyman is eternal, he exists as an inanimate being in all societies and comes to life when called upon by the aforementioned forces. When he is summoned, he is given form, and the public is warned of his presence—"be vigilant, the boogeyman is out to get you."

The Boogeyman

Many of us recall childhood stories like Little Red Riding Hood and Hansel and Gretel. The images and emotions that such stories evoked in us as children may be seared in our memories as adults. Indeed, fairy tales serve an important social function beyond childhood—namely deterrence, largely through fear. Our purpose here is not to discuss the benefits or harms of such stories but to acknowledge the function that fairytales serve in a sociological sense. Many of these stories leave lasting impressions, and the utility of their longevity cannot be overlooked. As adults, we succumb to their influence unknowingly perhaps but with some frequency and success. Consider the well-known Boogeyman, a mythical creature devoid of physical appearance with an etymological origin sometime in the mid-19th century.[36] Often conceived of as a devil or goblin in its various manifestations around the world, the Boogeyman was used to scare children into compliance, to ensure that they would not misbehave. Indeed, the Boogeyman was quite useful as a deterrent as it may target a specific act or general misbehaviour, depending on what purpose needs serving, often based on a warning from the child's authority figure. The term 'Bogeyman' is sometimes used as a non-specific personification or metonym for terror.

What belies the fears of Earnest, Terrant, and Bowers is not the Muslim per se—they were responding to high fashion hate signals—informed by policy and media and reinforced by social media, Internet memes, and the shape-shifting boogeyman. Such is the utility of the boogeyman for the purveyors of hate—they merely clothe the skeleton with the flesh of a desired enemy and set him loose upon the public—those daring enough will face him, and the consequences are often tragic.

Criminologists tell us that homicide has the highest clearance rate because stranger homicides are rare and occur in less than 10% of all murders.[37] The killing of Muslims often falls into the stranger-to-stranger homicide category because it doesn't reflect a personal vindication of a wrong inflicted by the victim upon the assailant, rather it is merely the assailant's reaction to the impulses of high fashion hate. In instances of hate crimes such as the mass shootings in Christchurch, New Zealand, the direct victims are rarely the targets of the Islamophobe—terrorism is after all the propaganda of the deed—the message is clear to members of the victims' group: Be afraid, be terribly afraid!

Replacement ... Guilty as Charged

The most pernicious yet baseless conspiracies circulating the Internet regarding Muslims are that they seek to replace Western civilization. Giving fodder to such arguments of course is the recent rise of groups like ISIS (Islamic State in Iraq and Syria) who claim to represent all Muslims in a quest to replace secular regimes with a singular caliphate which will rule in accordance with God's commands—Sharia law! However, such claims about Islamic replacement of Western values predate ISIS. Moreover, recent findings on Muslim attitudes from around the world toward ISIS find that the overwhelming majority showed significant disdain for the group,[38] refuting any claim by the group to represent the *Ummah* (the collective body of the faithful). This reality played out in August 2021 when President Biden pulled American troops out of Afghanistan—scenes of devastated Afghanis clinging to the bottom of US Airforce planes as they cruised down the runways, and some falling to their deaths in an effort to leave the country, speak to the disillusionment that many of them had with the militant Islamist ideology of the Taliban.

The shooters who violated the sacred spaces of Jews, Muslims, and other minorities in recent years have a lingering fear—being replaced. What these shooters traffic in is no longer a fringe idea—it has gone mainstream—yet largely popular in right-wing circles. Speaking before colleagues at a House Foreign Affairs Committee meeting, Pennsylvania Republican Representative Scott Perry stated that "for many Americans, what seems to be happening or what they believe right now is happening is what appears to them is we're replacing national-born American—native-born Americans to permanently transform the landscape of this very nation." In similar fashion, but to a much larger audience, Fox News' Tucker Carlson made a similar retort stating:

> The left ... become literally hysterical if you use the term "replacement," if you suggest that the Democratic Party is trying to replace the current electorate ... with new people ... obedient voters, from the third world ... Because that's what's happening, actually ... Every time they import a new voter, I become disenfranchised as a current voter.[39]

Known commonly as "replacement theory" or "white genocide" demographic conspiracies assert that an active force—often a cabal of elites—yielding great power seeks to subvert and replace the white race in America and Europe. Replacement takes on many forms but is most prominent in multicultural and liberal immigration policies intended on diluting whiteness beyond recovery. The origins of demographic conspiracies are nebulous, but sources suggest that they date back to the early 20th century with eugenics and Nazi Germany. Prominent among these is the 1934 pamphlet produced by the Research Department for the Jewish Question entitled "Are the White Nations Dying?"[40] More recently, in his fiery 1968 speech in Britain titled "Rivers of Blood," Enoch Powell warned the British public of an imminent takeover by an increasing influx of immigrants into the United Kingdom, echoing fears of his xenophobic predecessors. Contemporary offshoots are Bat Ye'or's *Eurabia: The Euro-Arab Axis* and Renaud Camus' *The Great Replacement* (2011) which argue that Europeans are being replaced by mass migration.[41]

As we have suggested early on in this book, simply trying to discredit a conspiracy theory places one within its causal framework—one becomes a nefarious agent sent to undermine the "truth." Consider for a moment the rationalizations that a conspiratorial mind would conjure: "just look at what demographers are saying about Spanish becoming the fastest growing non-English language in the United States," or "look up the names of many of the leaders of media companies or banks and you'll find that they're Jewish." The conspiracist may be correct, but they don't account for why these things happen—they're not astute students who recognize the complexities of a changing world due to mass migration, war, geopolitical issues, and most basic among these is a sociological maxim which holds that multicultural societies experience intergroup changes as a need to harness power, or to push back against prejudice and exclusion. A caveat—though many Jews (and Muslims) enter into fields such as media and finance, they don't do so merely to represent their group—there's a possibility that like most people, they don't think much about their racial identities when they're seeking out career opportunities—suggesting otherwise is no less troubling than the alternative—it homogenizes and essentializes the group.

We are befuddled by a particular irony about the shooters' indictment of Jews and Muslims as acting subversively—and at times in concert—to replace the white race. Indeed, the very accusation of an overthrow is evidence of white supremacy—it suggests an existing control structure which requires toppling. Could this be an admission of guilt from the shooters and their ilk? Rarely is the accusation of replacement met with a logical question—if we (Jews and Muslims) are replacing you (the white supremacist), what gives *you* the right to reign supreme? This is an especially interesting observation when we consider that often, white supremacists—let us be generous and say those of the mainstream variety—vehemently denounce the idea that white supremacy exists. They are partially correct—white supremacy lies obscure, hidden from plain sight. In her book *White Fragility: Why It's So Hard for White People to Talk about Racism*, Robin Diangelo tells us,

Racism is a structure, not an event. While hate groups that openly pro-
claim white superiority do exist and this term refers to them also, the
popular consciousness solely associates *white supremacy* with these
radical groups. This reductive definition obscures the reality of the
larger system at work and prevents us from addressing this system …
The United States is a global power, and through movies and mass
media, corporate culture, advertising, US-owned manufacturing, military presence, historical colonial relations, missionary work, and other
means, white supremacy is circulated globally. This powerful ideology
promotes the idea of whiteness as the ideal for humanity well beyond
the West.[42]

Citing Charles W. Mills' book *The Racial Contract*, Diangelo writes
that,

Mills describes white supremacy as the "unnamed political system
that has made the modern world what it is today." … Although white
supremacy has shaped Western political thought for hundreds of years,
it is never named. In this way, white supremacy is rendered invisible
while other political systems—socialism, capitalism, fascism—are
identified and studied … much of white supremacy's power is drawn
from its invisibility, the taken-for-granted aspects that underwrite all
other political and social contracts.[43]

Suffice it to say that such obvious questions to white supremacists as the
one we posit here must no longer go unanswered. The shooters assumed a
priori that *they* belonged while Jews and Muslims—and others deemed to
be intruders—did not. This claim is of course made throughout the shooters' manifestos, nearly without exception. But, could it be that the shooters
were merely using the fear of replacement as a pretext for their atrocities?
A motive that would justify their heinous acts and render themselves mar-
tyrs for a greater cause? We suspect that these shooters and conspiracists
like them aren't avid readers; they aren't attuned to the most recent scholarly publications of demographers. They did not concern themselves with
the filigreed theoretical matters relating to intergroup conflict—but were
merely looking for an excuse to live out their dream.

Notes

1 Frank Gaffney, Jr., accessed August 12, 2019, https://www.splcenter.org/fight-
ing-hate/extremist-files/individual/frank-gaffney-jr.
2 See, for example, "The Muslim Brotherhood Bogey Man," accessed December
26, 2016, http://huffingtonpost.com/scot-atran-muslim-bogey-men-egyp
817988.html. Also see Khalded Abou El Fadl, "How Hatred of Islam Is
Corrupting American's Soul," *Religion and Ethics*, January 19, 2017, accessed
January 21, 2017, http://www.abc.net.au/religion/articles/2017/01/18/4606049

.htm. and Georgi Ivanov, "Wanted: A New Bogeyman," accessed May 6, 2107, http://www.salon.com/2015/02/08/terrorisms_new_boogie_man_charles_krauthammer_and_the_toxic_myth_of_the_lone_wolf_partner/.

3 The nature of the MB was debated by a Congressional subcommittee see: 2018 The Muslim Brotherhood's Global Threat Hearing Before the Subcommittee on National Security of the Committee on Oversight and Government Reform House of Representatives One Hundred Fifteenth Congress Second Session July 11, 2018 Serial No. 115–90. Accessed February 22, 2020, https://docs.house.gov/meetings/GO/GO06/20180711/108532/HHRG-115-GO06-Transcript-20180711.pdf.

4 Bat Ye'or, *Eurabia: The Euro-Arab Axis* (Madison: Fairleigh Dickinson University Press, 2005).

5 "What Is the Muslim Brotherhood?," *Al-Jazeera*, last modified June 18, 2017, https://www.aljazeera.com/indepth/features/2017/06/muslim-brotherhood-explained-170608091709865.html.

6 Ibid.

7 Ibid.

8 Jesse Walker, "The Age of Frank Gaffney: War, Paranoia, and Institutional Power," last modified March 21, 2017, https://reason.com/2017/03/21/gaffney/.

9 Philip Bump, "Meet Frank Gaffney, the Anti-Muslim Gadfly Reportedly Advising Donald Trump's Transition Team," November 16, 2016. accessed August 8, 2019, https://www.washingtonpost.com/news/the-fix/wp/2015/12/08/meet-frank-gaffney-the-anti-muslim-gadfly-who-produced-donald-trumps-anti-muslim-poll/?noredirect=on.

10 Eric Hoffer, *The True Believer: Thoughts on the Nature of Mass Movements* (New York: Harper Collins, 2002).

11 *The Muslim Brotherhood Project*, accessed June 15, 2021, https://www.investigativeproject.org/documents/687-the-muslim-brotherhood-project.pdf.).

12 Ibid.

13 Ibid.

14 "Factsheet: The NYPD Muslim Surveillance and Mapping Program," *Bridge: A Georgetown University Initiative*, May 11, 2020, https://bridge.georgetown.edu/research/factsheet-the-nypd-muslim-surveillance-and-mapping-program/.

15 Tahir Abbas, "Muslim Minorities in Britain: Integration, Multiculturalism and Radicalism in the Post-7/7 Period," *Journal of Intercultural Studies* 28, no.3 (2008): pp. 287–300.

16 "Terrorism Attacks," *Ash Center for Democratic Governance and Innovation*, February 2016, accessed May 14, 2021, https://ash.harvard.edu/terrorism-attacks.

17 Australian Curriculum, "Australian curriculum: Aboriginal and Torres Strait Islander Histories and Cultures," accessed May 10, 2021, https://www.australiancurriculum.edu.au/media/1536/guiding-principles.pdf.

18 Amazon, "Eurabia: The Euro-Arab Axis," *Amazon*, accessed May 15, 2021, https://www.amazon.com/Eurabia-Euro-Arab-Axis-Bat-Yeor-ebook/dp/B004FN2C40.

19 Mark J. Perry, "New 2018 FBI Data: Jews were 2.7x More Likely Than Blacks, 2.2x More Likely than Muslims to Be Hate Crime Victim," *American Enterprise Institute*, November 13, 2019. https://www.aei.org/carpe-diem/new-2018-fbi-data-jews-were-2-7x-more-likely-than-blacks-2-2x-more-likely-than-muslims-to-be-hate-crime-victim/.

20 Damaris Graeupner and Alin Coman, "The Dark Side of Meaning-Making: How Social Exclusion Leads to Superstitious Thinking," *Journal of Experimental Social Psychology* 69 (March 2017): p. 218.
21 Bat Ye'or, *Eurabia*, p. 9.
22 James Loeffler, "The Problem with the Judeo-Christian Tradition," *The Atlantic*, August 1, 2020, https://www.theatlantic.com/ideas/archive/2020/08/the-judeo -christian-tradition-is-over/614812/.
23 Bat Ye'or, *Eurabia*, p. 9.
24 Ibid.
25 Ibid., p. 10.
26 Eleanor Beardsley, "France Considers a Law to Curb What It Views as Islamist Extremism." *NPR*, November 26, 2020, accessed June 15, 2021, https://www .npr.org/2020/11/26/939367415/france-considers-a-law-to-curb-what-it-views -as-islamist-extremism.
27 "Why Countering Violent Extremism Programs Are Bad Policy," *Brennan Center*, September 9, 2019, accessed June 15, 2021, https://www.brennancenter .org/our-work/research-reports/why-countering-violent-extremism-programs -are-bad-policy.
28 Ahmed had taken apart a clock and placed it in a briefcase to show to his high school engineering teacher. The teacher reported Ahmed for allegedly bringing in a bomb. (See: Wikipedia, "Ahmed Mohamed Clock Incident," 2015, accessed June 4, 2021, https://en.wikipedia.org/wiki/Ahmed_Mohamed_clock_incident.)
29 Edward W. Said, *Orientalism*, First edition (New York: Pantheon Books, 1978).
30 Arub Kundani, *The Muslims Are Coming! Islamophobia, Extremism, and the Domestic War on Terror* (London: Verso, 2014).
31 Khaled A. Beydoun, *American Islamophobia: Understanding the Roots and Rise of Fear* (Oakland: University of California Press, 2018).
32 "United States. Cuban Refugee Program," *University of Miami Libraries*, accessed June 9, 2021, https://atom.library.miami.edu/united-states-cuban-refu gee-program.
33 William L. Mitchell, "The Cuban Refugee Program," *Social Security Bulletin* (1962): pp. 3–8, accessed June 9, 2021, https://www.ssa.gov/policy/docs/ssb/ v25n3/v25n3p3.pdf.
34 For a detailed analysis of the process of assimilation, see: Amin Asfari, and Anas Askar, "Understanding Muslim Assimilation in America: An Exploratory Assessment of First and Second-Generation Muslims Using Segmented Assimilation Theory," *Journal of Muslim Minority Affairs* 40, no. 2 (2020): pp. 217–234.
35 Jack G. Shaheen. *Reel Bad Arabs: How Hollywood Vilifies a People* (Adlestrop, UK: Arris, 2003).
36 "Bogeyman," *Wikipedia*, last modified May 24, 2021, https://en.wikipedia.org/ wiki/Bogeyman.
37 Expanded Homicide, "FBI-UCR," accessed June, 12, 2021, https://ucr.fbi.gov/ crime-in-the-u.s/2017/crime-in-the-u.s.-2017/topic-pages/expanded-homicide.
38 Jacob Poushter, "In Nations with Significant Muslim Populations, Much Disdain for ISIS," November 17, 2015, accessed June 18, 2021, https://www.pewre search.org/fact-tank/2015/11/17/in-nations-with-significant-muslim-popula tions-much-disdain-for-isis/.
39 Chris Cillizza, "How the Ugly, Racist White 'Replacement Theory' Came to Congress," *CNN Politics*, April 15, 2021, https://www.cnn.com/2021/04/15/

politics/scott-perry-white-replacement-theory-tucker-carlson-fox-news/index
.html.
40 Paul Stocker, "The Great Replacement Theory: A Historical Perspective," *Open Democracy*, September 19, 2019, https://www.opendemocracy.net/en/countering-radical-right/great-replacement-theory-historical-perspective/.
41 Ibid.
42 Robin Diangelo, *White Fragility: Why It's So Hard for White People to Talk about Racism* (Boston: Beacon Press, 2018), pp. 28–29.
43 Ibid., p. 29.

4 Living the Dream

> I'd rather die in glory or spend the rest of my life in prison than waste away knowing that I did nothing to stop this evil. It is not in my blood to be a coward.
>
> John Earnest (Convicted of shooting worshipers in a California synagogue and setting fire to a mosque—sentenced to life imprisonment.)[1]

Normal Dudes

What possessed men who called themselves "normal dudes," men such as John Earnest, Robert Bowers,[2] and Brenton Tarrant[3] to murder worshipers in synagogues and mosques? We're not certain—certainty is for conspiracists. We may, however, have a piece of the puzzle. We suspect that anticipatory anxiety, not antecedent conditions, accounts for the shooters' actions—namely two anxious fixations:

- Changing demographics: Due to the secret machinations of a Jewish cabal, white Europeans face extinction—"white genocide."
- Recognition hunger: The shooters were not anonymous lone wolves. On the contrary, they craved adulation from their virtual community of anon bros (anonymous brothers).

Which fixation took priority? The shooters themselves might not know. We cannot, however, rule out what's hidden in plain sight: Their behavior suggests an insatiable craving for recognition. They couldn't stop immigration, but acclaim was forthcoming for these videogamers if they dared to risk everything and attained the highest kill score. This chapter reveals how we arrived at this unsettling prospect.

DOI: 10.4324/9781003207894-4

We began by rejecting the hackneyed rabbit hole metaphor. The shooters who massacred worshippers did not tumble down a rabbit hole—the centerpiece, of Lewis Carroll's *Alice in Wonderland*. They didn't encounter the amazing, peculiar characters in Alice's reverie. Tropes from a delightful children's story don't capture the bewilderment and the horror. We sought a more telling metaphor appropriate for fallen men acting out of character.

John Earnest, by far the most perplexing, claims that: "I'm just a normal dude, who wanted to have a family, help and heal people, and play piano."[4] False modesty: Actually, he was a cultured, accomplished young man. Chopin's Scherzo No. 2 was his favorite piano piece—he won prizes for his renditions. He also wanted to burn Muslims and Jews to death with a flamethrower—so he boasted. Earnest claims he was inspired by Bowers, who murdered Jews in Pittsburgh, and by Tarrant, who murdered Muslims in Christchurch, New Zealand.

Bowers and Tarrant also insist that they too are "ordinary white guys"— those who knew them agree. It is difficult, however, not to ruminate about Earnest: What we know of him is particularly baffling. Judging from his background, he would seem to be the least likely person to commit despicable acts: an honors student, scion of an ideal, progressive family, a religious young man training for a medical career—a son who would make any parent proud—till his downfall.[5] In an open letter, his distraught family grieved: "To our great shame, he is now part of the history of evil that has been perpetrated on Jewish people for centuries. How our son was attracted to such darkness is a terrifying mystery to us."[6]

His downfall recalled a myth retold in Plato's *Republic*—perhaps a cautionary tale: Anyone can fall through the cracks and plunge into a haunted, eerie space and be led into temptation. We learn of "The Ring of Gyges" in *Book Two*:

> Gyges, a shepherd boy, falls through a crevice following an earthquake and comes upon a skeleton wearing a ring. Upon wearing the ring, Gyges discovers a twist bestows invisibility. He uses the newfound power to seduce the queen, kill the king and assume his throne. Another twist and he's a formidably visible tyrant.[7]

However, before following the parable to where it leads—namely to the shooters' websites and to their deranged acts—we were duly diligent. We engaged in an obligatory search for deep-seated antecedent causes of the shooters' terror—the search proved futile.

The Conventional Wisdom

Investigators continue the search for the antecedent conditions that precipitate mass murder. A recent Department of Justice (DOJ)-funded study analyzed predisposing conditions—it proved largely irrelevant to our concerns. We couldn't check most of the DOJ boxes with one exception— the shooters had easy access to firearms. However, for the most part, the predisposing conditions listed by the DOJ didn't explain the shooters' heinous deeds; indeed, the deranged acts of a fine young man like John Earnest remain a "terrifying mystery."[8]

Unlike the murderers discussed in the study, the shooters were not victims of abusive families or bullies. They had nothing personal against Jews and Muslims—they didn't know any. They didn't compete with Jews and Muslims for jobs, housing, or other benefits.[9] Curiously, despite the vitriol heaped upon Jews and Muslims, no names were mentioned—not a word about a Rothschild or a Soros, or about a bin Laden or Baghdadi. Uninhibited by knowledge about Jews and Muslims, the shooters gave free rein to an unhinged imagination.

The social sciences, of course, continue to inquire into the antecedents of hatred and violence. These inquiries may prove productive, but current accounts were, at best, of limited value in accounting for the deranged behavior of these "ordinary dudes." At one extreme, Freudians attribute violence to unresolved Oedipal fixations.[10] (We cannot psychoanalyze the shooters; we can't tell whether they "say one thing but mean their mothers.")

On a more serious note, in struggling to make sense of violent extremism cloaked in conspiracist trappings, investigators sometimes default to extremes to make a point—the incongruous advent of Nazism. The culture that gave so much to the sciences and humanities embraced Hitler; Jews such as Freud and Einstein fled for their lives. Social scientists, as is their wont, give weight to socioeconomic factors. Taking a more granular, individuated approach, some analysts assign primacy to character traits such as the "authoritarian personality" to explain the most egregious, rightwing fanaticism.

Sociological Antecedents—Socioeconomic Status

A recent publication of the American Psychological Association (*Violence and Social Status*[11]) reviews the literature on the relationship between socio-economic conditions and abhorrent behavior. No surprises: The review finds strong correlations between poverty, discrimination, inadequate healthcare, poor education, high crime areas—and dysfunctional personalities. In short, deplorable socioeconomic conditions strongly correlate with future violence.

The harrowing circumstances of the Weimar Republic are an extreme case. Having lost the Great War, subject to Allied reparations—to say nothing of domestic corruption and mismanagement—ordinary Germans were impoverished, sickly, and hopeless. (The rate of inflation remains the stuff of legend.) Amid the Great Depression a once vibrant Berlin sank into a dystopia of despair—fertile grounds for Nazi recruiting. However, to understate the case, Tarrant's Australia and Bowers' America bore no semblance to Weimar Germany. Once again, Earnest proves particularly puzzling. Thriving in a nurturing, prosperous environment in the California sunshine, he partook of abundant opportunities, excelled in the classroom, gave piano recitals, swam on the school team, and enjoyed family and friends—not a page out of Weimar dystopia.

The Authoritarian Personality

During the 1950s much attention was given to a daunting question: How could otherwise law-abiding Germans, enjoying the hallmarks of Western civilization, become Nazis? Other nations endured bad times amid the Great Depression but didn't embrace fascism. Why was fascism irresistible? (Not a purely academic concern as the recent uptick in hate crimes and the storming of the Capitol illustrate.). Theodore Adorno and his colleagues moved in for a closer look and offered influential research regarding personality traits that may predispose individuals to the signature of fascism—the authoritarian personality.[12]

The authors concluded that authoritarian personalities result from rigid, if not cruel, child-rearing practices. Such unfortunate antecedents beget a rigid, binary worldview hostile to alternative viewpoints. This character type exalts power and demeans critical thought, adheres to conventional values, engages in bifurcated thinking, and cannot abide complex, ambiguous realities. In this authoritarian cartoon world, bright lines separate good from evil—no gray areas. We wouldn't be surprised to learn that Bowers and Tarrant endured unhappy, authoritarian childhoods, but certainly not Earnest. In any case, authoritarian personalities are not necessarily destined to act-out violent, conspiracist fantasies.

Updated commentary on the authoritarian personality detects ambiguities germane to our study. This personality type venerates power and exalts transgressive leadership—Trump comes to mind. Sociologist Chad Alan Goldberg analyzes the possibility that the adoration of power encourages disparaging hallowed tradition. Many supremacists idolized Donald Trump in their writings and musings because, as Goldberg suggests, contrary to the usual authoritarian predilections, he mocked customs and conventions.

Indeed, Adorno and his associates also noted ambiguities—if not contradictions—in their depiction. They suggested that the "authoritarian home regime" produces ... an "underlying resentment against ... authority and social institutions." This ambivalence explains why researchers often found in their "high-scoring subjects' traits of over conformity *and* of underlying destructiveness toward established authority and its mores and institutions." The authors of the classic work suggest that authoritarian personality's adherence to conventional values is determined exclusively by "external social pressure." But *"if permitted to do so by outside authority," the authoritarian person "may be induced very easily to uncontrolled release of his instinctual tendencies, especially those of destructiveness"* [ital. ours].[13]

The January 6, 2021, invasion of the Capitol is painfully relevant. Supremacist groups such as the Proud Boys dutifully lauded the police in their rhetoric and vilified Black Lives Matter for undermining law and order. Even so, they trashed the Capitol and attacked police. The shooters, of course, violated the most sacred norms by murdering innocent congregants in their sanctuaries. Nevertheless, they somehow felt justified—self-defense against Jewish and Muslim malevolence.

A consensus emerges among those who have investigated these men: The shooters *are* as ordinary as they claim; their backgrounds are (Earnest's accomplishments aside) unremarkable.[14] We realized that we hadn't exhausted the search for antecedent factors, a search that must continue. However, we decided to pursue a neglected tact: Giving anticipatory anxiety its appropriate place in accounting for the shooters' deranged acts. The shooters were addicted to a literal operant conditioning regime that traffics in anticipatory anxiety—a regime known as the Internet. They couldn't take their eyes off the screen.

Returning to the parable, we imagine Our Candidate—desperate for all-consuming conspiracist passion—hooked on the Internet. Like Gyges, he falls into a bizarre world in which he can be an unknown, invisible user, *or* a brazenly visible pusher of memes and red pills. (The old channels used by the shooters, venues such as 4chan and 8chan have changed their names to protect the guilty. Newer platforms such as Gab, YouTube, Instagram, and the upstart Telegram are readily available.[15]) Starting with these channels, we followed the path that leads men seeking meaning and recognition to arson and murder. We begin with their Internet addiction that climaxes in performative violence.

Internet Addiction

Addiction is not limited to vulnerable individuals predisposed to destructive compulsions—antecedent conditions do not always account for such dependency. A stable individual treated for back pain may become yet another statistic in the opioid epidemic. A person wastes a few dollars on a slot machine in Vegas: Unfortunately, what happens in Vegas doesn't always stay in Vegas. Like Gyges, the "normal dudes" fell through the cracks into an eerie, highly addictive cyberspace featuring an irresistible attraction: They could be invisible malefactors—doxxers and trolls, *or* brazenly visible edgelords spreading contagious memes, pushing red pills, or live-casting, performative violence.

Perhaps Earnest's vertiginous plunge into violent conspiracism was not accidental. Could it be that he sought out cracks in his near-perfect, seamless world? (Was Dostoevsky even more insightful than usual when he defined a human being as something that walks on two legs and feels ungrateful?) Dreading an all-too-conventional, uneventful future, was he enticed by the forbidden: notorious conspiracist websites, venues that would be anathema to his wholesome family—the main attraction perhaps? He dealt with temptation by giving in to hate-mongering, supremacist sites.

Turning to these sites, we note the irony: Members of the virtual brotherhood bantered about make-believe conspiracies, while an actual conspiracy shamelessly manipulated them behind their backs. The sites were plotted to get them hooked. As novelist Julia Bell observes: In a "kind of joyless behaviorism—humans [are] reduced to the calculus of an algorithm."[16] To ensure ongoing addiction, companies rely upon random reinforcement through clickbaits and algorithms to sustain interaction. Hooked on what comes next, addicts can't take their eyes off the screens. Likening such tactics to drug dealing isn't merely metaphorical: Addicts build up tolerance as they are fed more content—more potent fixes guarantee dependence. Well-tuned algorithms provide a constant high.

The shooters were hooked by the sites' mesmerizing spectacle of nonstop white supremacist rallies—no censorship, no gatekeeping, no inhibition. Such rallies galvanize a virtual community rewarding anonymous subscribers (anon bros) with immediate gratification for giving free rein to the id—what could be more addictive?[17] Robert Bowers (the shooter who terrorized the Pittsburgh synagogue) just couldn't get enough pixilated hatred: "In the 19 days before he carried out his act of mass murder, [11 worshipers in a Pittsburgh synagogue] he posted or reposted memes and comments at least 68 times."[18] Mind viruses—memes—infected his mind.

Immersed in this unhinged postmodern cyberspace, Our Candidate need not struggle to interpret classics such as the *Protocols*. No one wastes precious audience attention by posting ponderous texts—unlike Nilus they don't bore potential recruits. In effect, the white supremacist theology inscribed in canonical works such as the *Protocols* and *Eurabia* is deconstructed, torn asunder into amusing memes, racist slurs, vile in-jokes, and unhinged fantasies—those promoting these sites pray the laughter is contagious.

Thanks to the Internet, the Ring of Gyges became postmodern magic. A click and the addict remains an invisible "anon bro" (anonymous brother);

another click and he's a visible player. It's fun and addictive. Invisibility has its advantages, but it's poor optics for those craving recognition. Addicts may make a name for themselves through malevolence-signaling or by breaking taboos—Holocaust jokes are always cringe-worthy. Our Candidate may even aspire to become an edgelord by pushing intoxicating red pills filled with the shards of bygone conspiracy theories, or by devising and spreading contagious mind viruses—intoxicating memes.

Memes: The Shards of Bygone Conspiracy Theory

Arguably, Spanish isn't the fastest-growing non-English language in the United States—it's the language of memes. Today, it's the short video, the quick photo, the snappy phrase—in short, the meme. Anyone with access to the Internet can create memes. But not all memes are created equal; some go viral, others wither and die. Tracing the etymology of the term, Jeremy Burman explains: "When the meme" was introduced in 1976, it was a metaphor intended to illuminate an evolutionary argument. By the late 1980s, however, we see from its use in major US newspapers that this original meaning was obscured. The meme had become a *virus of the mind*" [ital. ours].

Postmodern Internet sites are about entertainment. Posting, nuanced, extended arguments is worse than useless; it's boring—an unforgiveable infraction—too much like school or a dull evening with PBS when visiting grandparents. The postmodern conspiracist eschews critical inquiry, let alone grandiloquence. On their go-to sites, works such as the *Protocols*, *Eurabia*, and *The Great Replacement*[19] are reduced to memes: inflammatory kindling for incendiary violence.[20]

Not only do the postmodernists keep it simple, they invoke the lulz—transgressive entertainment to keep normies cringing. Memes move through the Internet with speed and accuracy, seldom detected due to their unassuming nature. They're often humorous—survival of the funniest. Many, of course, are loathsome, trafficked by wannabe edgelords—who offer something to offend everyone. Trolls relish the lulz—schadenfreude. Like graffiti scrawled in sacred spaces, vile memes are meant to be seen and abhorred by normies. They're pushed in those dark alleys of the Internet where only the addicted reside—sites like 8kun, 4kun, Gab, and the dark recesses of the Internet.[21]

Memes mocking Jews and Muslims marked the Trump era—permission granted to defame out-groups. Taking the analysis further, Gold and Shanks direct attention to a particularly pernicious artifact—the conformity meme. These "mind viruses" reinforce existing beliefs, promote homogenized thinking, and impede critical thought—alternative perspectives are eliminated a priori. Such memes prompt the user to express views favored by other subscribers facilitating the contagion—not unlike a gene replicating a phenotypic trait. Contagion occurs beyond cyberspace. A user infected by these mind viruses may join a rally, affix bumper stickers, and harass neighbors and officials.

Because conformity memes render their hosts unable—or unwilling—to consider alternative viewpoints, they undermine core values of civil society, a culture that ideally promotes a civic engagement and the free exchange of ideas. Multicultural practices are anathema to white supremacists who are not above invoking the old-fashioned red scare. Multiculturalism is maligned as "cultural Marxism" by those who probably never read a shred of Marxist text.

Those who revel in these memes are not noted for temperate, reasoned discourse; their ad hominems target enemies real and imagined. Supremacists abide by *their* version of what is politically correct—namely, disparaging the other. Bowers *was* politically correct in referring to the caravan of asylum seekers from Honduras and El Salvador "illiterate brutal murderers," and to Jews as "kikes" infesting America (i.e., Replacement Theory). Tarrant refers to non-whites in Europe (most often to Muslims) as "rapists" and "non-white scum" as well as "invaders." And in the gospel according to Earnest (at the time a member in good standing of the Presbyterian Faith) Christian pacifists honoring peacemakers and praying for enemies are an abomination perpetrated by Jews. No kind words for Christian brethren who "trust yids and their puppet braindead lemming normal fags to falsify the Gospel."[22]

Much to the chagrin of white supremacists, Jews generally pass for generic white. Stereotypes turn the ordinary to other. The title of literary critic Josh Lambert's book review says it all: "Taking it on the Nose: A Fresh Look at Cartoon Jews and Anti-Semitism."[23] The author alludes to an experiment in which children were asked to draw a Jew; most of the stick figures had rather prominent "toucan noses." Turning to cartoons and popular memes, there are no surprises: Jews are depicted as leering, lecherous, greedy, and—to be sure—plotting evil deeds.

What of Muslims? A Saudi in traditional garb is readily identifiable. But what of a Chechen, Bosnian, or a fair-skinned Circassian Turks? The supremacist imagination mirrors the meme proliferating in the 24/7 white supremacist online rallies.

Memeification of Islamophobia

Islamophobic memes reflect the social beliefs that permeate society at a given time, and they construct new realities. Because memes are broadly constructed as ideas, behaviors, or styles as defined by Dawkins, they encompass more than contemporary still images found on the Internet. Our more expansive notion includes depictions of Muslims in film, still photography, drawings, literature, and—to be sure—television. We locate Muslim memes on a historical continuum from pre- to post-9/11—Muslims shape-shift from magician to monster.

In some instances, the varieties of othering converge and appear in a singular depiction, a seemingly benign Orientalism. Consider the classic 1960s sitcom, aptly named *I Dream of Jeannie*; the star is a scantily clad blonde woman played by Barbara Eden who is also a 2000-year-old genie. The pilot episode previews:

> Astronaut Captain Tony Nelson['s] ... capsule comes down [on] a deserted island... . Tony notices a strange bottle ... When he rubs it ... a Persian-speaking female genie materializes and kisses Tony on the lips ... Tony expresses his wish that Jeannie could speak English.[24]

Figure 4.1 Publicity photo of Larry Hagman and Barbara Eden from *I Dream of Jeannie*. Source: Press release is undated but lists the episode as being aired September 18. There is a date stamp for September 7, 1965. The show premiered September 18, 1965. NBC Television, Public domain, via Wikimedia Commons (https://en.wikipedia.org/wiki/File:I_dream_of_jeannie_hagman_eden.JPG).

Sociologist Erving Goffman's analysis suggests the title signifies a dream, a mirage sought but never attained. The genie appeals to an American audience played by a blonde, white female. The Orientalist gaze fixates upon an attractive haram-like woman from a place where women are sexualized—not unlike the Western audience consuming the unfolding comedy. The American astronaut—with his advanced technological mind—finds himself nonetheless baffled by the unfamiliar foreign tongue of the genie— "Persian," (Farsi) an unmistakable association with the Near East: She's commanded to adopt his ways by speaking English—the subservient must please their masters!

In a process known as "keying" Goffman articulates an interpretive frame analysis[25] whereby the audience's frame of reference is drastically altered in revolutionary fashion. Looking to our Hansel and Gretel fairy tale metaphor, we see this transformation in the witch who lures children inside the home: The kindly old woman shape-shifts into the blood-thirsty cannibalistic version of herself once the children are trapped. Likewise, post-9/11 "The Arab" is transformed through popular depictions and memes: The fabled, magical exotic becomes the omnipresent boogeyman.

Figure 4.2 Terrorists. Source: Jadejanandraja, May 22, 2020, CC BY-SA 4.0, via Wikimedia Commons (https://commons.wikimedia.org/wiki/File: Terrorists.jpg).

The conspiracists' highly addictive websites do not merely display viruses—malevolent memes about Jews and Muslims. As we'll see—particularly in the case of Earnest—these viruses infect and replicate themselves in a once healthy mind. Virulent memes multiply exponentially and make the website experience raucously thrilling, entertaining, and addictive. *The memes are kindling.* We sought the spark that inflamed the shooters.

The Denouement

Prior to committing their atrocities, would-be heroes posted on their favored sites to boast of their plans while burnishing their reputations. We view their postings and manifestos with suspicion. Indeed, how shall we interpret the words and the deeds that followed? Our interpretations may well reveal more about us than the shooters—happily, far removed from our personal and professional lives. Chastened, we hazard a plausible interpretation of the shooters' atrocities.

Given our suspicions, we are not convinced their manifestos reveal the demons driving these "regular white dudes." In this post-Freudian world, were the shooters themselves cognizant of their motives? As Geertz quipped, we seldom understand the guy in that office down the hall—let alone ourselves. Even if the shooters knew what made them tick, why assume their candor? Did they really hate Jews and Muslims or were they just "talking the talk"—the price of admission? Could it be that they wrote what was needed for peer acceptance and acclaim? We weren't certain about what to believe and what to reject out of hand. All that said, amid these humbling circumstances we attend to the shooters' deeds—perhaps they're telling.

We note a curiosity: Rather than invoking their usual memes, quips, and vile attempts at irony, the shooters' manifestos invoked serious discourse—the permanence and authority of the typographic text. (Earnest and Tarrant authored full-fledged manifestos; Bowers wrote a few paragraphs prior to his deranged deed.) In these texts, the shooters, of course, rail against imagined enemies, but there's a subtext: The manifestos read like a last will and testament. Perhaps the manifestos are furtive quests for ersatz immortality? Like the feckless Hamlet, are the shooters crying out "Remember Me!" To paraphrase Earnest Becker's hauntingly powerful *Denial of Death*, could it be that the shooters' anticipated heroic projects camouflaged naked despair? Becker won't let us forget that, in our dress-up charade, *we* forget—for a time—that we're imposters pretending to be immortal rather than animals fated to rot in the ground.[26]

Turning to this world, Earnest's newfound community seemed terribly significant to him. He entreated them:

> The true anons out there (you know who you are). You are the product of ... unadulterated truth. You are my brothers and the best dudes out there. You are the most honorable men of this age. Despite all odds against you, you not only discovered the truth but also help to spread it.[27]

Bowers, driven by a fanatic's pressing urgency—had no time for a brush with immortality. There were exigencies: annihilating the Jews and Muslims who would—in his imaginary—replace, if not exterminate, white Europeans. As we've seen, on their go-to sites, works such as the *Protocols*, *Eurabia*, and *The Great Replacement*[28] were reduced to fragments and innuendo—highly inflammable kindling.[29]

What did the shooters expect? Their manifestos expressed the fervent hope that their heroism would inspire others to join the cause—stop white genocide by killing Jews, Muslims, and other minorities. This was wishful thinking; did they know it? None of the previous acts of domestic terrorism fomented the race war they longed for—no "Day of the Rope" when their enemies would be publicly hanged. However, their behavior suggests that they pinned their hopes on an immediate triumph; their heart's desire was within reach—achieving the highest kill count.

Gamification

Gamification turns a non-game experience into a fun-filled game.[30] Such highly addictive games (think playing slot machines euphemistically called "gaming") motivate participation, engagement, and loyalty with three elements: points, badges, and rewards. Relying upon emerging studies of gamification, we analyze the fatal attraction of the shooters' gamification. Schlegel suggests that the "live-streaming of attacks, the use of *Call of Duty* footage in propaganda videos, the modification of popular video games to support extremist world views, and the development of games ... by extremist organizations have all contributed to an increasing focus on the ... 'gamification' of terror."[31]

In this way, it can be argued that games became a template for conspiracist thought and action: in gamified space, Jews and Muslims were not of ordinary flesh and blood; they were akin to villains vanquished in their favored pastime—videogames such as *Call of Duty: Modern Warfare*. In this action-packed, first-person shooter game, good guys with amazing weapons hunt and kill bad guys—some of the episodes depict the War on Terror in the Greater Middle East. One reviewer "loved" the amazingly realistic sound of gunfire. Another: "Absolutely loved the campaign. It was immersive and gives real attachment to the characters. The vast selection of weapons and their attachments never get boring."[32]

This gamification of conspiracist terrorism represents the latest advance in their authorial strategy. Initially, conspiracist communicated in by forging the *Protocols*. Realizing, perhaps, that their potential recruits had little appetite for sustained reading, they resorted to transgressive metaphors: Jews were likened to rodents; Muslims to a malignancy in the body politic. Memes, as we've seen, traffic in cringe-worthy depictions of despised groups. Conspiracism, while increasingly entertaining, remained passive amusement, a spectator sport—until the recent advent of gamification.

Gamification (the métier of QAnon) doesn't merely provide a ringside seat; it's interactive. Players are rewarded with a sense of accomplishment as they win badges and acclaim. Addicts may suspend disbelief and imagine themselves as macho-psychotic warriors. Tarrant, as we've seen, was well aware of the enticement. The *Protocols*—definitely not the product of a fun-loving century—panders fear. Gamified conspiracism is about fun and play—competing for the highest kill score. Players also get to score others: In various sites: "Scoreboards rank the success of far right perpetrators ... who have expressed the desire to beat [Tarrant's] score." The Nazi site, *Stormfront*, encourages participants to "play" genocide, and it replays its gamified version of Tarrant's Christchurch massacre.[33]

The shooters' manifestos express the fervent hope that their heroism will inspire others to prevent white genocide by killing Jews, Muslims, and other minorities: Wishful thinking and they likely knew it; they allowed that their actions might fail. However, they pinned their hopes on an immediate triumph; their heart's desire—achieving the highest kill score. Game on!

The conspiracists' deeds suggest that acclaim—especially the adulation of their anon bros—took precedence, over a glorious cause. The postmodern detritus on the shooters' websites—vile in-jokes, ugly slurs, and cringe-worthy memes, and the like—provided kindling. An audacious challenge sparked incendiary violence. A dedicated fanatic, solely devoted to a cause, wouldn't need prodding: He'd act anonymously on his own—a mysterious lone wolf committing heinous crimes in darkness. He wouldn't broadcast his actions as a public, livestreamed spectacle—in short, he wouldn't want to get caught. Earnest and Tarrant, seem driven by venality; they responded to a dare—a gauntlet thrown by themselves (in Tarrant's case) or by anon bros—who were not above humiliating their brethren. One way or another, the three shooters dared comrades to: stop shitposting, live the heroic dream, prove their manhood, shoot up a synagogue or mosque—and become an immortal by winning the highest kill score![34]

Fearless Bowers, as we'll see, staged a public spectacle in his imagined combat zone—the Pittsburgh Tree of Life Synagogue. Moving in for a closer look at the manuscripts, we contrast thought and deed. We begin with the most recent incident, Earnest's attack on a suburban San Diego synagogue, and look backward to his acknowledged indebtedness to the crimes of Tarrant and Bowers. We'll start with the self-congratulatory narcissism of John T. Earnest who chose his parents wisely.

Earnest Manifesto

> The Jew has forced our hand, and our response is completely justified.
>
> John T. Earnest[35]

A dedicated terrorist would not call attention to himself by publicly posting a manifesto celebrating his plans. Earnest's manifesto begins by reciting the litany of white supremacist theology. As we've seen, he venerates himself and his ennobling English, Nordic, and Irish heritage—biology being destiny. One, with a bloodline such as he, is to be celebrated for his inherited "bravery, ingenuity, and righteousness." He was fond of quoting Scripture, as are we: "Ye shall know them by their deeds." He vowed he would "die a thousand times over to prevent the doomed fate that the Jews have planned for my race."[36] He did not tempt fate; he chose not to die at all.

In his manifesto, he insists he sought neither fame nor glory. His deeds belie such humility. He boasted online about vying for the highest kill score, went public, and livestreamed his synagogue atrocity. It takes a flair for the obvious to recognize that a dedicated terrorist—who cared only about the cause—would adorn the Ring of Gyges and remain invisible. He certainly would not boast about his "brave" plans on the Internet, nor advise followers about how to increase their kill scores in a game played for the highest stakes. A true fanatic dedicated to the cause, would not think of himself. He'd twist the ring, become invisible, act surreptitiously, and perhaps secretly plant explosives. He wouldn't burst into a synagogue firing a rifle; livestreaming a mission is the last thing an effective terrorist would do—if he cared enough about the cause to live to fight another day. Contrary to his vows, Earnest wasn't willing to die for a cause, but he was eager to seek acclaim. He, and he alone, had to burnish his reputation and stand above the rest—an inspiration to all.

He set fire to a mosque under cover of night—effective terrorism. (Fortunately, the inhabitants escaped unharmed.) But he revealed his insatiable recognition of hunger by bursting into a synagogue, opening fire upon worshipers who meant him no harm and killing one worshipper while injuring others—including the rabbi. Shortly thereafter, despite his oaths, he peacefully surrendered to authorities to whom he thoughtfully revealed his location. Finally, amid his trial, he plea-bargained to avoid the death penalty.

It's as if Earnest were involved in a videogame writ large. An anon bro dared Earnest to live the dream. The taunts continued even after Earnest announced his heroic dream: "The very first reaction to Earnest's post on 8chan announcing his plan was a user urging him to get a high score."[37] His dream became a nightmare to worshippers in the suburban San Diego synagogue. Earnest burnished his reputation with a twist of the Ring. He became starkly visible, not only by posting his plans but also by posting tips for attaining the highest kill score—the prized 8chan commodity. Like Tarrant, he hoped to gain everlasting fame by livestreaming his rampage. He failed. Feckless Earnest was ridiculed for merely attaining a single kill—no honor among thieves or conspiracists.

Earnest may have believed that, despite his caution, the manifesto might be his last words. He offered a benediction: "Brothers in blood. Make sure that my sacrifice was not in vain. Spread this letter, make memes ..." He eulogizes the immortals who courageously battled before him by killing helpless worshipers: "FIGHT BACK, REMEMBER ROBERT BOWERS, REMEMBER BRENTON TARRANT."[38]

Remembering Brenton Tarrant

In his manifesto, Tarrant insisted that he had no desire for recognition. His behavior belies such false modesty. Enthralled by videogames, Tarrant craved a record number of kills: he garnered praise as the top killer; adulation as a knight or saint. It seems he had such adulation in mind upon orchestrating a production made for primetime—livestreaming a massacre accompanied by a musical score, belies such false modesty. He boasts that: "I did not attend University [*sic*] as I had no great interest in anything offered." Like the other shooters, Tarrant got his xenophobia from Replacement Theory shattered into shards on 8chan—more kindling for the ensuing inferno: "[I] received, researched, and developed my beliefs, from the internet, of course. You will not find the truth anywhere else."[39] And yet, the lengthy manuscript begins with poetic lines from Dylan Thomas and from Rudyard Kippling as he takes up the white man's burden, and goes into that good night.

Tarrant also credited his travels with his radicalization. He witnessed Muslims profaning white spaces in every French city he visited. He saw French military cemeteries—wooden crosses stretched to the horizon. He allows that he "broke into tears, sobbing alone, staring at the forgotten dead." Finally, he laments that brave soldiers will have died in vain if the Muslim invaders are allowed to overcome us "without a single shot fired in response." (But somehow his English ancestors were justified in invading and conquering his native Australia.)

It seems that Tarrant suffered a loss of reality. The fallen French soldiers, of course, were slain by Germans, fellow very white Europeans, in world wars, not by Muslims. He realizes that his courageous fight against Muslim invaders may well lead to prison. Expressing the apotheosis of the supremacist imagination: he's confident that, like Nelson Mandela, the time will come when he's released, and celebrated for saving his people—an imagined Nobel Peace Prize awaits.

His response to an online comment reveals his mental status, at once troubling and delusional. Apparently, a strident critic called him "a bigot, racist, xenophobe, islamophobe, nazi, fascist." At first, he joked, "compliments will get you nowhere." But apparently, the accusation tweaked raw nerves bringing on a grand mal catharsis. We'll spare the reader and only cite but a few passages that bespeak a loss of reality no longer garnished with poetry:

> What the fuck did you just fucking say about me, you little bitch? … I graduated top of my class in Navy seals … I'm the top sniper in the entire US armed forces. You think you can get away saying that shit to me over the Internet? … I am contacting my secret network of spies across the USA … I have access to the entire arsenal of the United States Marine Corp … you're fucking dead, kiddo.

However, the manifesto from the Australian who imagines soldiering above all others in the US military is not without medieval chivalry: Noblesse oblige, he thanked "Knight Justicar Breivik" for blessing his proposed project—murdering unarmed Muslims as they worshipped in Christchurch, New Zealand. (Knighthood was in flower when Breivik massacred scores of Norwegian children.)

Venturing onto these sites, one enters a maisma of video gamers with its peculiar argot, a realm strewn with the trivial pursuits of popular culture. 4chan and 8chan began as venues for videogames and quickly became the go-to sites for conspiracists under the spell of videogames. Tarrant gives credit where credit is due. He anticipates a bro's question: "Were you taught violence and extremism by video games, music, cinema? Yes, Spyro the dragon 3 taught me ethno-nationalism. Fortnite trained me to be a killer and to floss on the corpses of my enemies."[40]

Like the other shooters, Tarrant imagines that a conspiracy is underway and must be stopped. The Western World (overrun with swarthy immigrants in the supremacist's imagination) no longer resembles a 1950s Norman Rockwell, *Saturday Evening Post* cover. And it's happening as they watch: The all-white world of primetime television is no more. Tarrant in near-panic warns: "The 10000-ton boulder of demographic change rolls ever forward, gaining momentum and possibly destroying all in its path."[41] The take-home lesson of the *Protocols* reverberated in bizarre, pixilated form for the self-proclaimed, anticipated victims of the Great Replacement—exterminate or be exterminated!

As we saw in Chapter 1, Tarrant envisioned his site as more than a mere message board. It was a recruitment tool. A catalyst for a community that would "promote the warmth and genuine love we have for our people."[42] The overwhelming majority of his Australian and New Zealand people condemned Tarrant's degenerate deed. Even so, he inspired the likes of John Earnest.

Becoming an anonymous brother provided a false sense of community and a seemingly receptive audience. But, like Gyges, Internet addicts could not abide everlasting invisibility. Making matters worse, many of the so-called bros found gratification and delight in the lulz: ridiculing and humiliating comrades—easy targets. They taunted one another. To paraphrase typical refrains: Quit shitposting and have the balls to do something! Who is man enough to take on the burden of the race and stop the kikes and ragheads? *This became the flashpoint.* The shooters' narcissism was their undoing. Tarrant ignited the spark within himself. His bold letters were emphatic: "WHY WON'T SOMEBODY DO SOMETHING? WHY DON'T I DO SOMETHING? The spell broke, why don't I do something?"[43]

Earnest boasted that he too was up to the challenge. In the shooters' make-believe world of dress-up charades, "Doing something" means imagining yourself as a medieval knight or a Norse warrior crusading against perfidious Jews and Muslims. (Earnest promised he would meet his anon bros in Valhalla.)

Tarrant craved a record number of kills: he garnered praise as the top killer; adulation as a knight or saint.

Commenting upon Tarrant's Christchurch atrocities, *New York Times* reporter Warzel explains:

> In these [online] communities after Christchurch there was [an] outpouring of people saying you know this shooter got a high number of kills ... something like in a video game ... Who can top the high score? ... People are essentially just waiting to see whether or not they've beaten the last act of terrorism, whether or not they've gotten a high score ... glorifying those who do ... chastising those who don't.[44]

Robert Bowers' Postings

Neighbor Chris Hall told AP: "The most terrifying thing is just how normal he [Robert Bowers] seemed."[45]

On October 27, 2018, Robert Bowers burst into the Tree of Life Synagogue bellowing "All Jews must die!" He murdered 11 worshippers—an unprecedented massacre of American Jews. He had no criminal record, except for a minor infraction—expired tags on his truck. Writing for the Southern Poverty Law Center (SPLC) Alex Amend emphasizes that Bowers was likely radicalized entirely online. (Apparently, Bowers had no personal contact with Jews; like Tarrant his beliefs about Jews were derived online—not from the "Jew-controlled" media.) Gab and other sites echoed Trump's dire warning about the invasion nearing America's southern border. In vintage conspiracist style, Bowers connected the dots between two fictions: Jewish malevolence and the pending invasion of dangerous alien races from the south.

Jews were not his only fetish. He frequently posted homage to guns and to his treasured collection. One indelible image featured three displays of weaponry—his "Glock Family." (Grist for the Freudian mill!) Guns and paranoia became a fatal mix that sabbath day. Upon killing congregants, Bowers was wounded in an exchange of gunfire with the local SWAT team. Transported to Allegheny General Hospital, he told SWAT Operator David Blahut that he wanted all Jews to die: They were committing genocide to his people.[46] Ari Mahler, a Jewish nurse who initially treated him and likely saved his life, recognizes the irony, how could he not: "I'm sure he had no idea I was Jewish. Why thank a Jewish nurse, when 15 minutes before, you'd shoot me in the head with no remorse?"[47]

His postings on Gab—a favorite site of the most fanatical white supremacists—focused upon three themes: white genocide, nativism, and globalization. He echoed the paranoid claim of other users: The Hebrew Immigration Aid Society (HIAS)—a long-established nonprofit that aids all immigrants—was bringing in immigrants bent upon displacing Americans of European origin; worse yet, the immigrants were criminals intent upon rape and murder. Without citing evidence, he posted: "HIAS likes to bring invaders that kill our people."[48]

Trump, of course, promoted comparable claims. His followers had somehow determined that George Soros, a Holocaust survivor and benefactor of progressive causes, promoted the invasion. He was accused of condoning, if not instigating, white genocide. Even so, Bowers, as we've seen, despised Trump for inviting a Jew, Jared Kushner, into his family. Indeed, he claimed that Jewish globalists—international financiers—controlled Trump. As Bowers posted, there could be no MAGA (Make America Great Again) amid a "kike invasion."

The effluvia of the *Protocols* are evident in Bowers' postings. The Jews (a seamless cabal scheming for world domination) controlled the Zionist Occupied Government (ZOG), the media, and promoted multiculturalism to encourage miscegenation thereby further diminishing the white population. Behind the scenes, a slow genocide was occurring due to interracial marriages, and a lower birth rate among whites of European heritage. In one of his postings Bowers imagined that Jews have nothing better to do than to wage a propaganda war against Western civilization, a war so effective that we whites will be extinct in 200 years—most are clueless about what lies ahead.[49]

And in his dress-up charade Bowers was a make-believe fearless soldier throwing caution to the wind by taking-on fire in the killing fields. "I can't sit by and watch my people get slaughtered. Screw your optics. I'm going in."[50] Of course, like the others, he chose his target very carefully: He didn't "go in" against Jewish soldiers or police. Helpless congregants in Pittsburgh tested his mettle.

An Afterword

Examples of white supremacist conspiracism proliferate. Unhappily, instances of true believers denouncing conspiracism and lamenting the error of their ways are few and far between. As we've seen epistemological vigilantes seldom persuade conspiracists to abandon their paranoid fantasies. Indeed, such attention is welcomed oxygen for conspiracists.

Personal experience is more compelling than homiletics about the evils of conspiracism. The good news, of course, is that informal, personal contact with Jews and Muslims often alleviates prejudice. The bad news is that such contact is not on the supremacists' agenda. However, not all experience need to be salutary to be life changing. On the contrary, *betrayal* by comrades and by venerated heroes has an indelible impact.

Betrayal

The case of Mike Fanone, a 40-year-old Capitol Hill police officer, is instructive. Featured on the cover of *Time Magazine*, he testified before the House Committee investigating the events of January 6, 2020.[51] He learned more than he cared to about the insurrection—fellow Trump supporters nearly killed him.

Like those who besieged him, Mike was enthralled by Trump's bombastic personality, expressed patriotism, and selective enthusiasm for law and order—he voted for Trump. Mike fervently believed that Trump's nemesis, members of the "radical left," were cop-hating, unamerican miscreants, and much worse. On that fateful January day, amid the siege, he was accosted by fellow Trump supporters and beaten with "thin blue-line" flags. His taser was taken and used against him: beaten and sprayed repeatedly, he testified that he narrowly escaped death.

Following his recovery and testimony, he received much support from liberals, and condemnation from conservative pundits—self-professed champions of law and order. Indeed, Fanone's contemporaries, police officers, once called friends, sent memes mocking *his* betrayal![52] Fanone declared "The greatest trick in history was Donald Trump convincing redneck Americans that he somehow speaks for them.... He will destroy this country for the sake of his ego." His message to them and others who are spellbound by Trump—wake up! Speaking of his ordeal in hindsight, he allows: "What if I had not gone through that? ... I'd be the same dumbass that I was on Jan. 5. Not evil in my intentions. But ignorant to the truth."[53]

Finally, we circle back and return to the fate of QAnon Shaman and his epiphany: He expected Trump would pardon him; it was not to be. He did get the international recognition he craved while trashing the Capitol. His 15 minutes of shame ends with a whimper, not a bang. He might not relish the recognition he receives as he serves his 41 months prison sentence.

Notes

1 *edailybuzz.com/2019/04/28/*john-earnest-manifesto, accessed August 13, 2019. On September 30, 2021, Earnest was sentenced to life in prison without parole. Hereafter referred to as "Earnest Manifesto."

2 See Robert Bowers' Manifesto, "Analyzing a Terrorist's Social Media Manifesto...," accessed August 20, 2019, https://www.splcenter.org/hatewatch /2018/10/28/analyzing-terrorists-social-media-manifesto-pittsburgh-synagogue -shooters-posts-gab. Rev. Mark Schollaert, a minister who knew Bowers, describes him as: "normal there was never any unkindness or negativity." Accessed November 11, 2019, https://www.washingtonpost.com/national/pitts-burgh-shooting-suspect-left-fleeting-impression-in-neighborhoods-he-lived-in -for-decades/2018/10/31/90e1250c-dd44-11e8-b732-3c72cbf131f2_story.html.

3 Tarrant's Manifesto, "The Great Replacement," accessed November 8, 2019, https://www.bing.com/videos/search?q=tarrant+manifesto%2c+the+great +replacement&&view=detail&mid=8FF4.

4 Earnest Manifesto.

5 In the aftermath of Earnest's attack on the suburban San Diego synagogue, Julie Zauzmer Weil raised a troubling question in her *Washington Post* feature, "The alleged synagogue shooter was a churchgoer who talked Christian theology, raising tough questions for evangelical pastors," accessed November 26, 2021, https://www.washingtonpost.com/religion/2019/05/01/alleged-syna-gogue-shooter-was-churchgoer-who-articulated-christian-theology-prompting -tough-questions-evangelical-pastors/. Earnest, according to his pastor, was a devout member of a Presbyterian congregation. However, Presbyterians were not expected to account for atrocities committed by a congregant. By way of contrast, when a Muslim commits such a crime, it's deemed a thematic feature of Islam—Muslims better explain!

6 Quoted in the *Los Angeles Times*, April 30, 2019, accessed September 11, 2022 ("Troubling portrait of synagogue shooting suspect emerges: 'Attracted to such darkness,'" 2019).

7 Plato, *The Republic, Book Two*, trans. Alan Bloom (New York: Basic Books, 1968).

8 VICE Blog, accessed November 21, 2019, https://www.vice.com/en_us/article/a35mya/nearly-all-mass-shooters-since-1966-have-had-four-things-in-common. Unlike the typical mass shooters, the three terrorists didn't suffer from an abused childhood, school bullies, or personal crises, nor were they harassed, let alone injured, by Jews and Muslims.

9 United States Department of Justice, "General Methodology," *Gun Violence Archive*, accessed June 19, 2019, https://www.gunviolencearchive.org/methodology. In a seemingly insignificant exception: According to his posting, Tarrant was enraged when a person identified as Muslim bought a store's, last videogame, a game he longed to have.

10 See, for example, "The Trauma and Disillusionment of Oedipus," 99, no. 3, accessed September 12, 2022, https://www.tandfonline.com › ... ›

11 "Violence and Socioeconomic Status," *Fact Sheet: American Psychological Association,* accessed November 24, 2021, https://www.apa.org/pi/ses/resources/publications/factsheet-violence.pdf.

12 Theodore Adorno et al., *The Authoritarian Personality* (London: Verso, 2019).

13 See Chad Alan Goldberg, "Authoritarians Amok: Explaining Trumpism, with Some Help from Chad Goldberg and Herbert Marcuse," *Altercation*, accessed September 26, 2021, http://americanprospect.activehosted.com/index.php?action=social&chash=a9b7ba70783b617e9998dc4dd82eb3c5.1051&s=34b b44f2660dbeb7ad5b70af2029af22..

14 See, for example, VICE Blog, accessed November 21, 2019, https://www.vice.com/en_us/article/a35mya/nearly-all-mass-shooters-since-1966-have-had-four-things-in-common. Christopher Browning's *Ordinary Men* comes to mind. Amid World War II, Polish police joined the occupying Nazis in murdering Jews. However, the shooters were not under control of an occupying army. They did, however, succumb to the peer pressure of their cherished virtual community.

15 After Tarrant livestreamed his Christchurch massacre on 8chan, the site was shut down temporarily and reopened as 8kun. See April Glaser, "Where 8channers went after 8chan," *Slate,* November 11, 2019, accessed December 9, 2021, https://slate.com/technology/2019/11/8chan-8kun-white-supremacists-telegram-discord-facebook.html. Also See Kevin Roose, "Shut the Site Down, 'Says the Creator of 8chan, a Megaphone for Gunmen,'" *New York Times,* August 4, 2019, accessed December 7, 2021, http://www.nytimes.com/2019/08/04/technology/8chan-shooting-manifesto.html. 8chan was reincarnated as 8kun. Bowers posted on Gab—site still in business. Conspiracists also use YouTube. The upstart *Telegram* sites is the latest venue for antisemitic conspiracism. See, Gian Volpicelli, "Telegram Is Becoming a Cesspool of Anti-Semitic Content," *Wired*, October 13, 2021, accessed December 7, 2021, https://www.wired.com/story/telegram-becoming-cesspit-antisemitic-content.

16 Julia Bell, *Radical Attention* (London: Peninsula Press, 2020), p. 77.

17 Walter Isaacson, who ate dinner with the Jobs family while researching his biography of Steve Jobs, told [*New York Times* reporter John] Bilton that, "No one ever pulled out an iPad or computer. The kids did not seem addicted at all to devices." Quoted by Alter, 2. Alter quips: "It seemed as if the people producing tech products were following the cardinal rule of drug dealing: never get high on your own supply."

18 Alex Amend, Southern Poverty Law Center Hate Watch Site, accessed November 15, 2019, https://www.splcenter.org/hatewatch/2018/10/28/analyzing-terrorists-social-media-manifesto-pittsburgh-synagogue-shooters-posts-gab.

19 Renaud Camus, *You Will Not Replace Us* (Paris: Chez Auteur, 2017).
20 We're indebted to Joseph E. Uscinski and Joseph M. Parent, *American Conspiracy Theories* (Oxford, New York, et al.: Oxford University Press, 2014) for this telling "kindling/ignition" metaphor.
21 As previously mentioned, Tarrant and Earnest posted manifestos on 8chan and 4chan and tried to use these sites to livestream their atrocities. The sites were briefly taken down and renamed.
22 Earnest Manifesto.
23 Josh Lambert, "Taking It on the Nose: A Fresh Look at Cartoon Jews and Anti-Semitism," *Haaretz*, August 1, 2017, accessed December 15, 2021, "Taking It on the Nose: A Fresh Look at Cartoon Jews and Anti-Semitism."
24 Wikipedia, "I Dream of Jeannie," June 8, 2021, accessed June 18, 2021, I Dream of Jeannie - Wikipedia.
25 Erving Goffman, *Frame Analysis: An Essay on the Organization of Experience* (Boston: Boston University Press, 1974).
26 Earnest Becker, *The Denial of Death* (New York: Free Press, 1973), p. 58.
27 Earnest Manifesto.
28 Camus, *You Will Not Replace Us*.
29 We're indebted to Uscinski and Parent's *American Conspiracy Theories*, for this telling "kindling/ignition" metaphor.
30 See Adam Alter, *Irresistible: The Rise of Addictive Technology and the Business of Keeping us Hooked* (New York: Penguin Publishing Group, 2018).
31 Linda Schlegel, *The Role of Gamification in Radicalization Process* (Berlin: Centre for Applied Research on Deradicalization, January 1, 2001), accessed September 12, 2022.
32 *Call of Duty: Modern Warfare*, accessed September 12, 2022, https: call+of+duty+modern+warfare&sxsrf=ALiCzsZu_v2LftguJsMWfavejMckhqc9XQ%3A1663002879270&source=hp&ei=_2gfY8zzCpPUkPIP8N2TKA&iflsig=A JiK0.
33 Schlegel, *The Role of Gamification in Radicalization Process.*
34 Investigative reporters from the mainstream press also entertain this possibility. See Georgia Wells and Ivan Lovett, "So What's His Kill Count?…" *Wall Street Journal*, accessed November 8, 2019, https://www.wsj.com/articles/inside-the -toxic-online-world-where-mass-shooters-thrive-11567608631; we're indebted to our correspondence with Wells. We profited from Charlie Warzel's analysis in: "The Gamification of Domestic Terrorism Online," *PBS Newshour*, August 4, 2019, accessed November 14, 2019, https://www.pbs.org/newshour/show/the -gamification-of-domestic-terrorism-online.
35 Earnest Manifesto.
36 Ibid.
37 Charles Warzel, "The Gamification of Domestic Terrorism Online," *PBS Newshour*, October 15, 2019, accessed November 18, 2019, http://www.pbs.org /newshour/show/the-gamification-of-domestic-terrorism-online.
38 Earnest Manifesto.
39 Tarrant Manifesto. The veracity of Tarrant's site is self-evident—at least to him.
40 Tarrant Manifesto. Of course, not every videogamer becomes a terrorist. We'll suggest that, in the cases of Tarrant and Earnest, the gamer mentality was a necessary, *but not sufficient*, condition. Bowers, evidentially, was not obsessed with gaming. The shards and constant reinforcement from the anon bros may have been enough to set him off.

41 Ibid.
42 Manifesto, "The Great Replacement."
43 Ibid.
44 Warzel, "The Gamification of Domestic Terrorism Online," *PBS Newshour*, August 4, 2019.
45 Quoted in "Pittsburgh Synagogue Gunman Suspect: Who Is Robert Bowers?" *BBC NEWS*, October 28, 2018, "The Most Terrifying Thing Is Just How Normal He Seemed," accessed November 10, 2018, https://www.bbc.com › world-us-canada-46022930.
46 https://www.splcenter.org/hatewatch/2018/10/28/analyzing-terrorists-social -media-manifesto-pittsburgh-synagogue-shooters-posts-gab.
47 Ari Mahler, "I am the Jewish Nurse," *Nurse Organization*, Fall 2021, accessed December 21, 2021, https://nurse.org/articles/Jewish-nurse-treated-synagogue -shooter/.
48 Quoted by Alex Amend, Southern Poverty Law Center, *Hate Watch*, October 28, 2018. The white supremacists' appropriation of the term "genocide" is starkly ironic and unnerving. The term, as we've seen, was coined by Raphael Lemkin, a Jewish lawyer: It referred to the systematic, deliberate, attempted extermina- tion of an entire ethnic or racial group—the fate of European Jews during World War II.
49 Ibid.
50 See "What's Known about Robert Bowers," accessed November 25, 2019, https://www.npr.org/.../whats-known-about-robert-bowers-the-suspect-in -the-pittsburgh-oct 27, 2018. Also see Wells and Lovett, "So What's His Kill Count?..."
51 Molly Ball, "What Mike Fanone Can't Forget," *Time*, August 5, 2021, accessed October 24, 2021, https://time.com/6087577/michael-fanone-january-6-interview/.
52 Ibid.
53 Ibid.

Bibliography

Abbas, Tahir. 2008. "Muslim Minorities in Britain: Integration, Multiculturalism and Radicalism in the Post 7/7 Period." *Journal of Intercultural Studies* 28(3): 287–300.

Adorno, Theodore, Else Frenkel-Brunswik, Daniel J. Levinson, and Nevitt R. Sanford. 2019. *The Authoritarian Personality*. London: Verso.

Al Jazeera Staff. 2017. *What Is the Muslim Brotherhood?* June 18. https://www.aljazeera.com/features/2017/6/18/what-is-the-muslim-brotherhood.

Amend, Alex. 2018. *Analyzing a Terrorist's Social Media Manifesto: The Pittsburgh Synagogue Shooter's Posts on Gab*. October 28. Accessed August 20, 2019. https://www.splcenter.org/hatewatch/2018/10/28/analyzing-terrorists-social-media-manifesto-pittsburgh-synagogue-shooters-posts-gab.

Asfari, Amin, and Anas Askar. 2020. "An Exploratory Assessment of First and Second-Generation Muslims Using Segmented Assimilation Theory." *Journal of Muslim Minority Affairs* 40: 217–234.

Atran, Scott. 2011. *The Muslim Brotherhood Bogey Man*. February 2. Accessed December 26, 2016. https://www.huffpost.com/entry/the-muslim-bogey-men-egyp_b_817988.

———. n.d. *Australiam Curriculum: Aboriginal and Torres Strait Islander Histories and Cultures*. Accessed May 10, 2021. https://www.australiancurriculum.edu.au/media/1536/guiding-principles.pdf.

Baddiel, David. 2015. *Short of a Conspiracy Theory? You Can Always Blame the Jews*. July 22. https://www.theguardian.com/commentisfree/2015/jul/22/conspiracy-theory-jews-david-cameron-antisemitism-extremism.

Ball, Molly. 2021. *What Mike Fanone Can't Forget*. August 5. Accessed October 4, 2021. https://time.com/6087577/michael-fanone-january-6-interview/.

Bangstad, Sindre. 2013. "Eurabia Comes to Norway." *Islam and Christian-Muslim Relations* 24(3): 369–391.

Beardsley, Eleanor. 2020. *France Considers A Law to Curb What It Views as Islamist Extremism*. November 26. Accessed June 15, 2021. https://www.npr.org/2020/11/26/939367415/france-considers-a-law-to-curb-what-it-views-as-islamist-extremism.

Bell, Julia. 2020. *Radical Attention*. London: Peninsula Press.

Berger, J. M. 2019. *The Dangerous Spread of Exremist Manifestos*. February 26. https://www.theatlantic.com/ideas/archive/2019/02/christopher-hasson-was -inspired-breivik-manifesto/583567/.

Beydoun, Khaled A. 2018. *American Islamophobia: Understanding the Roots and Rise of Fear*. Oakland: University of California Press.

Bezalel, Glenn. 2021. "Conspiracy Theories and Religion: Reframing Conspiracy Theories as Bliks." *Episteme* 18(4): 674–692.

Bloom, Alan, trans. 1968. *Plato, the Republic, Book Two*. New York: Basic Books.

Bottum, Joseph. 2003. *Disenchantment and Its Discontents: Why Catholics Need Not Choose Between Science and Wonder*. Accessed October 29, 2021. https:// www.thenewatlantis.com/publications/disenchantment-and-its-discontents.

Bridge Initiative Team. 2020. *Factsheet: The NYPD Muslim Surveillance and Mapping Program*. May 11. https://bridge.georgetown.edu/research/factsheet -the-nypd-muslim-surveillance-and-mapping-program/.

Brotherhood. n.d. *Investigative Project*. Accessed June 15, 2021. https://www.inv estigativeproject.org/documents/687-the-muslim-brotherhood-project.pdf.

Brotherton, Rob. 2017. *Suspicious Minds*. Kindle Edition. London: Bloomsbury.

Brotherton, Robert, and Eser Silan. 2015. "Bored to Fears: Boredom Proneness, Paranoia, and Conspiracy Theories." *Personality and Individual Differences* 80: 1–5.

Bump, Philip. 2016. *Meet Frank Gaffney, the Anti-Muslim Gadfly Reportedly Advising Donald Trump's Transition Team*. November 16. Accessed August 8, 2019. https://www.washingtonpost.com/news/the-fix/wp/2015/12/08/meet-frank -gaffney-the-anti-muslim-gadfly-who-produced-donald-trumps-anti-muslim -poll/?noredirect=on.

Burtt, E. A. 2003. *The Metaphysical Foundations of Modern Science*. Moneola: Dover.

Camus, Renaud. 2017. *You Will Not Replace Us*. Paris: Chez Auteur.

———. 2018. *The Great Replacement*. Paris: Chez l'Auteur.

CDC. n.d. *The U.S. Public Health Service Syphylis Study at Tuskegee*. Accessed May 21, 2021. https://www.cdc.gov/tuskegee/timeline.htm.

Chomsky, Noam. 2002. *Distorted Morality: America's War on Terror*. February. https://chomsky.info/200202__02/.

Cillizza, Chris. 2021. *How the Ugly, Racist White 'Replacement Theory' Came to Congress*. April 15. https://www.cnn.com/2021/04/15/politics/scott-perry-white -replacement-theory-tucker-carlson-fox-news/index.html.

Cohn, Norman. 1957. *The Pursuit of the Millennium*. Fairhaven: Essential Books.

Conspiracism. n.d. *Lexico*. Accessed January 5, 2022. https://www.lexico.com/ definition/conspiracism.

Contributors, Wikipedia. 2021. *Ahmed Mohamed Clock Incident*. June 4. https:// en.wikipedia.org/w/index.php?title=Ahmed_Mohamed_clock_incident&oldid =1048289386.

Contributors, Wikipedia. 2022a. *Beavis and Butt-Head*. January 6. Accessed September 24, 2021. https://en.wikipedia.org/wiki/Beavis_and_Butt-Head.

Contributors, Wikipedia. 2022b. *Bogeyman*. January 7. https://en.wikipedia.org /w/index.php?title=Special:CiteThisPage&page=Bogeyman&id=1064113830 &wpFormIdentifier=titleform.

———. n.d. *I Dream of Jeannie*. Accessed June 18, 2021. https://en.wikipedia .org/w/index.php?title=Special:CiteThisPage&page=I_Dream_of_Jeannie&id =1056374568&wpFormIdentifier=titleform.

David, Ariel, and Davide Lerner. 2019. *'Jesus Was Not a Jew!' Clueless REMark by Far-Right Politician Sparks Outrage in Italy*. December 4. Accessed September 11, 2021. https://www.haaretz.com/world-news/.premium-jesus-was-not-a-jew -remark-by-far-right-politician-sparks-outrage-in-italy-1.8204043.

Diangelo, Robin. 2018. *White Fragility: Why It's so Hard for White People to Talk about Racism*. Boston: Beacon Press.

Dowie, Mark. 1977. *Mother Jones*. September/October. Accessed April 30, 2021. https://www.motherjones.com/wp-content/uploads/v2n8_sept1977-pinto.pdf.

Earnest, John. 2019. *John Earnest Manifesto*. April 28. Accessed August 13, 2019. edailybuzz.com/2019/04/28/john-earnest-manifesto.

El Fadl, Khaled Abou. 2017. *Who's Afraid of the Muslim Brotherhood? How Hatred of Islam Is Corrupting the American Soul*. January 18. Accessed January 21, 2017. https://www.abc.net.au/religion/whos-afraid-of-the-muslim-brotherhood -how-hatred-of-islam-is-cor/10096150.

Eriksen, Erik. 2012. "The Protocols of the Elders of Mecca." *Interstate - Journal of International Affairs* 2: 1–21.

———. 2017. *Expanded Homicide*. Accessed June 12, 2021. https://ucr.fbi.gov/ crime-in-the-u.s/2017/crime-in-the-u.s.-2017/topic-pages/expanded-homicide.

Fernandez, Luke, and J. Susan Matt. 2021. *Bored, Lonely, Angry, Stupid: Changing Feelings about Technology, from the Telegraph to Twitter*. Cambridge: Harvard University Press.

Flint, Colin. 2004. *Spaces of Hate: Geographies of Discrimination and Intolerance in the U.S.A.* London: Routledge.

Ford, Henry. 2011. *The Protocols of the Meetings of the Learned Elders of Zion*. Translated by Victor E Marsden. Austin: RiverCrest Publishing.

Franks, Bradley, and Adrian Bangerter. 2003, July 16. "Conspiracy Theories as Quasi-Religious Mentality: An Integrated Account from Cognitive Science, Social Representation Theory, and Frame Theory." *Frontiers in Psychology* 4: 4.

———. n.d. *Frank Gaffney Jr.* Accessed August 12, 2019. https://www.splcenter .org/fighting-hate/extremist-files/individual/frank-gaffney-jr.

Galilieo, Brecht. 2010. *Unhappy the Land That Has No Heros*. February 6. Accessed August 12, 2019. https://www.kaieteurnewsonline.com/2010/02 /06/"unhappy-the-land-that-has-no-heroes.

Garner, Dwight. 2015. *Review: 'One of Us,' by Asne Seierstad, on Anders Breivik's Rampage in Norway*. April 9. https://www.nytimes.com/2015/04/10/books/ review-one-of-us-by-asne-seierstad-on-anders-breiviks-rampage-in-norway .html.

———. n.d. *General Methodology*. Accessed June 19, 2019. https://www .gunviolencearchive.org/methodology.

Ghose, Tia. 2013. *Surprise: Ashkenazi Jews Are Genetically European*. October 8. Accessed March 29, 2021. https://www.livescience.com/40247-ashkenazi-jews -have-european-genes.html.

Glaser, April. 2019. *Where 8channers Went after 8chan*. November 11. Accessed December 9, 2021. https://slate.com/technology/2019/11/8chan-8kun-white-supremacists-telegram-discord-facebook.html.

Goertzel, Ted. 2019. "The Conspiracy Theory Pyramid Scheme." In *Conpiracy Theories and the People Who Believe Them*, edited by Joseph E. Uscinski, Chapter 15, 226–244. London: Oxford University Press.

Goffman, Erving. 1974. *Frame Analysis: An Essay on the Organization of Experience*. Boston: Boston University Press.

Goldberg, Chad Alan. 2021. *Athoritarians Amok: Explaining Trumpism, With Some Help From Chad Goldberg and Herbert Marcuse*. Accessed September 26, 2021. http://americanprospect.activehosted.com/index.php?action=social&chash=a9b7ba70783b617e9998dc4dd82eb3c5.1051&s=34bb44f2660dbeb7ad5b70af2029af22. .

Goldfarb, Michael. 2009. *Emancipation: How Liberating Europe's Jews from the Ghetto Led to Revolution and Renaissance*. Kindle Edition. New York: Simon and Schuster.

Goodman, Brenda. 2020. *Cytokine Storms May Be Fueling Some COVID Deaths*. April 17. Accessed October 21, 2021. https://www.webmd.com/lung/news/20200417/cytokine-storms-may-be-fueling-some-covid-deaths.

Gopnik, Adam. 2009. *Trial of the Century*. September 28. Accessed October 3, 2021. https://www.newyorker.com/magazine/2009/09/28/trial-of-the-century.

Graeupner, Damaris, and Alin Coman. 2017. "The Dark Side of Meaning-Making: How Social Exclusion Leads to Superstitious Thinking." *Journal of Experimental Social Psychology* 69: 218.

Graves, Philip P. n.d. "The Truth about "the Protocols: A Literary Forgery: From the Times of August 16, 17, and 18, 1921." *WorldCat*. Accessed October 16, 2021. https://www.worldcat.org/title/truth-about-the-protocols-a-literary-forgery-from-the-times-of-august-16-17-and-18-1921/oclc/20045122.

Hayes, Chris. 2021. *The New Yorker*. September 24. https://www.newyorker.com/news/essay/on-the-internet-were-always-famous.

Heil, Jonathan. 2012. "Thomas of Monmouth and the Protocols of the Sages of Narbonne." In *The Paranoid Apocalypse: A Hundred-Year Retrospective on the Protocols of the Elders of Zion*, edited by Richard Landes and T. Stephen Katz, 56–78. New York: New York University Press.

Hentoff, Nat. 1985. *The Pariah*. June 22. Accessed April 29, 2021. https://www.washingtonpost.com/archive/politics/1985/06/22/the-pariah/cfeaf942-2e98-46a6-9d80-09b9a4ceda71/.

Hirschbein, Ron. 2016. "The Morbid Gaze: Terrorism as Entertainment." *Tikkun* 3(1): 44–48.

Hochberg, Gil Z. 2016. "'Remembering Semitism' or 'on the Prospect of Re-Membering the Semites'." *ReOrient* 1(2): 2.

Hoffer, Eric. 2002. *The True Believer: Thoughts on the Nature of Mass Movements*. New York: Harper Collins.

Hoffman, E Katherine. 2009. "Culture as Text: Hazards and Possibilities of Geertz' Literal/Literary Metaphor." *Journal of North African Studies* 14(3–4): 417.

Hofstadter, Richard. 1964. *The Paranoid Style in American Politics*. New York: Harpers.

Iambecauseweare. 2018. *Qanon–The Storm*. March 12. Accessed December 15, 2021. krypt3ia.files.wordpress.com/2018/08/q_s_posts_-_cbts_-_7-2-0.pdf.

Ingber, Sasha. 2019. *Alleged California Synagogue Shooter 'Part of the History of Evil,' His Parents Say*. April 30. Accessed December 11, 2021. https://www.npr.org/2019/04/30/718563232/part-of-the-history-of-evil-parents-say-of-alleged-california-synagogue-shooter.

Jacobson, Kenneth. 1981. "The Protocols: Myth and History." Accessed October 21, 2021 https://www.adl.org/sites/default/files/documents/assets/pdf/anti-semitism/united-states/the-protocols-myth-and-history-1981.pdf.

———. 2014. *Jewish Girl Was "Poster Baby" in Nazi Propaganda*. July 2. Accessed April 22, 2021. https://www.yadvashem.org/blog/jewish-girl-was-poster-baby-in-nazi-propaganda.html.

———. n.d. *Jean-Francois Lyotard*. Accessed September 27, 2021. https://iep.utm.edu/lyotard/.

Kaplan, Fred. 2005. *Let's Go to the Memo*. June 15. Accessed July 13, 2021. https://slate.com/news-and-politics/2005/06/what-s-really-in-the-downing-street-memos.html.

Katz, T. Steven. 2012. *A Hundred Year Perspective on the Protocols of the Elders of Zion*, edited by Richard Landes and T. Steven Katz. New York: New York University Press.

Keeley, L Brian. 1999. "Of Conspiracy Theory." *The Journal of Philosophy* 96(3): 120.

Kofman, Ava, Moira Weigel, and Francis Tseng. 2020. *White Supremacy's Gateway to the American Mind*. April 7. Accessed October 11, 2021. https://www.theatlantic.com/technology/archive/2020/04/white-supremacys-gateway-to-the-american-mind/609595/.

Kundani, Arub. 2014. *The Muslims Are Coming! Islamophobia, Extremism, and the Domestic War on Terror*. London: Verso.

Lakoff, George. 2003. *Metaphors We Live By*. Chicago: University of Chicago Press.

Lambert, Josh. 2017. *Taking It on the Nose? A Fresh Look at Cartoon Jews and Anti-Semitism*. April 24. Accessed December 15, 2021. https://www.haaretz.com/life/books/.premium.MAGAZINE-taking-it-on-the-nose-cartoon-jews-and-anti-semitism-1.5436537.

Levy, Richard S. 2021. "Setting the Record Straight Regarding the Protocols of the Elders of Zion: A Fool's Errant?" In *Nexus Two: Essays in German Jewish Studies*, edited by Williams Collins and Martha B Heller, 43–61. Camden: Boydell and Brewer.

Loeffler, James. 2020. *The Problem With the 'Judeo-Christian Tradition'*. August 1. https://www.theatlantic.com/ideas/archive/2020/08/the-judeo-christian-tradition-is-over/614812/.

Luban, David. 2021. *Hannah Arendt Meets QAnon: Conspiracy, Ideology, and the Collapse of Common Sense*. Accessed September 6, 2021. https.//scholarship.law.georgetown.edu/facpub/2384.

Mahler, Ari. 2018. *"I Am the Jewish Nurse"- RN Who Treated Synagogue Shooter Shares Story.* November 5. Accessed December 21, 2021. https://nurse.org/ articles/Jewish-nurse-treated-synagogue-shooter/.

Maly, Ico. 2019. "White Terrorism, White Genocide and Metapolitics 2.0." *Diggit.* Accessed December 20, 2021. https://pure.uvt.nl/ws/portalfiles/portal/50284907 /White_terrorism_metapolitics2.0_and_the_great_replacement_Diggit_ Magazine.pdf.

Marantz, Andrew. 2019. *Anti-Social Media: Online Extremism, Techno-Utopians, and the Hijacking of the American Conversation.* New York: Viking.

Marr, Wilhelm. n.d. "The Victory of Judaism over Germandom." *German History in Document and Images.* Accessed November 1, 2021. https://germanhistorydocs .ghi-dc.org/.

Marche, Stephen. 2022. *The Next Civil War: Dispatches from the American Future.* Kindle Edition. New York: Avid Reader Press/Simon & Schuster.

McEwen, Bill. 2021. *Have You Heard the One about Biden's Face on Trump's Body?* January 22. Accessed September 9, 2021. https://gvwire.com/2021/01/22 /have-you-heard-the-one-about-bidens-face-on-trumps-body.

Mishkov, Aleksandar. 2018. *Tuskegee Experiment–Fatal Conspiracy Theory Turned Out to Be True.* Accessed May 21, 2021. https://www.documentarytube.com/ articles/tuskegee-experiment-fatal-conspiracy-theory-turned-out-to-be-truth.

Mitchell, William L. 1962. "The Cuban Refugee Program." *Social Secutiry Bulletin* 25: 3–8.

Mohamed, Besheer. 2018. *New Estimates Show U. S. Muslim Population Continues to Grow.* January 3. Accessed September 20, 2012. https://www.pewresearch.org /fact-tank/2018/01/03/new-estimates-show-u-s-muslim-population-continues-to -grow/.

Muirhead, Russell, and Nancy Rosenblum. 2020. "Will Reality Bite Back: Conspiratorial Fictions and the Assault on Democracy." *The Forum* 18(3): 415–433.

Muirhead, Russell, and Rosenblum Nancy. 2019. *A Lot of People Are Saying.* Kindle Edition. Princeton: Princeton University Press.

Museum, United States Holocaust Memorial, Washington, DC. n.d. *The Elders of Zion: Key Dates.* Accessed October 10, 2021. https://encyclopedia.ushmm.org/ content/en/article/protocols-of-the-elders-of-zion.

Nagle, Angela. 2017. *Kill All Normies.* Alresford: Zero Books.

Noriega, David, and Tess Owen. 2019. *Nearly All Mass Shooters Since 1966 Have Had 4 Things in Common.* November 19. Accessed November 21, 2019. https:// www.vice.com/en_us/article/a35mya/nearly-all-mass-shooters-since-1966-have -had-four-things-in-common.

Perry, Mark J. 2019. *New 2018 FBI Data: Jews Were 2.7X More Likely than Blacks, 2.2X More Likely than Muslims to Be Hate Crime Victim.* November 13. https:// www.aei.org/carpe-diem/new-2018-fbi-data-jews-were-2-7x-more-likely-than -blacks-2-2x-more-likely-than-muslims-to-be-hate-crime-victim/.

Pew Research Center. 2021. *Jewish Americans in 2020.* May 11. Accessed September 20, 2012. https://www.pewforum.org/2021/05/11/the-size-of-the-u-s -jewish-population.

Pierce, William. 2019. *The Turner Diaries*. Mountain City: Cosmotheist Books.

Pitts, Leonard Jr. 2015. *20 Years after the Bombing in Oklahoma*. April 15. Accessed August 18, 2021. https://www.indystar.com/story/opinion/columnists/2015/04 /15/years-bombing-oklahoma/25859611/.

———. 2019. *Pittsburgh Synagogue Gunman Suspect: Who Is Robert Bowers?* October 29. Accessed November 10, 2018. https://www.bbc .com›world-us-canada-46022930.

Popper, Karl. n.d. *Goodreads Quotes*. Accessed August 29, 2021. https://www .goodreads.com/author/quotes/349707.Karl_Popper.

Postman, Neil. 1985. *Amusing Ourselves to Death: Public Discourse in the Age of Show Business*. New York: Penguin.

Poushter, Jacob. 2015. *In Nations With Significant Muslim Populations, Much Disdain for ISIS*. November 17. Accessed June 18, 2021. https://www .pewresearch.org/fact-tank/2015/11/17/in-nations-with-significant-muslim -populations-much-disdain-for-isis/.

Powell, Jim. 1998. *Postmodernism for Beginners*. Kindle Edition. Danbury: For Beginners LLC.

Prooijen, Jan-Willem, Joline Ligthart, Sabine Rosema, and Xu Yang. 2022. "The Entertainment Value of Conspiracy Theories." *British Journal of Psychology* 113(February): 25–48. Accessed August 27, 2022. https://resolver.scholarsportal .info/resolve/00071269/v113i0001/25_tevoct.xml.

Reimann, Nicholas. 2021. *QAnon Marked Friday as Trump 'Reinstatement' Day– Here Are Other Flop Predictions of Trump's Return*. August 13. Accessed August 30, 2021. https://www.forbes.com/sites/nicholasreimann/2021/08/13/qanon -marked-friday-as-trump-reinstatement-day-here-are-other-flop-predictions-of -trumps-return/?sh=2f70973a2a77.

Roose, Kevin. 2019. *Shut the Site Down, 'Says the Creator of 8chan, a Megaphone for Gunmen'*. August 4. Accessed December 7, 2021. http://www.nytimes.com /2019/08/04/technology/8chan-shooting-manifesto.html.

Rothschild, Mike. 2021. *The Storm Is Upon Us: How QAnon Became a Movement, Cult, and Conspiracy Theory of Everything*. Brooklyn: Melville Publishing.

Rudin, James A. 2014. *The Dark Legacy of Henry Ford's Anti-Semitism (Commentary)*. October 10. Accessed October 6, 2021. https://www.washingtonpost.com/ national/religion/the-dark-legacy-of-henry-fords-anti-semitism-commentary /2014/10/10/c95b7df2-509d-11e4-877c-335b53ffe736_story.html.

Said, Edward W. 1978. *Orientalism*. First Edition. New York: Pantheon Books.

Sant, Shannon Van. 2018. *What's Known about Robert Bowers, the Suspect in the Pittsbugh Synagogue Shooting*. October 27. Accessed November 25, 2019. https://www.npr.org/2018/10/27/661409410/whats-known-about-robert-bowers -the-suspect-in-the-pittsburgh-synagogue-shooting.

Security, Subcommittee on National. 2018. *The Muslim Brotherhood's Global Threat*. Government Report, Washington, DC: U.S. Government Publishing Office.

Shaheen, Jack G. 2003. *Reek Bad Arabs: How Hollywood Vilifies a People*. Adlestrop: Arris.

Sikander, Sana. 2020. *Oklahoma Bombing: When Arabs Were Blamed for Homegrown Attack.* April 20. Accessed July 11, 2021. https://www.siasat.com/oklahoma-bombing-when-arabs-were-blamed-homegrown-attack-1876918/.

Smith, Stephen B. 2006. *Modernity and Its Discontents.* New Haven: Yale University Press.

Spencer, Richard Bertram. n.d. *Southern Poverty Law Center.* Accessed September 22, 2021. https://www.splcenter.org/fighting-hate/extremist-files/individual/richard-bertrand-spencer-0.

Steiner, John. 2018. "The Trauma and Disillusionment of Oedipus." *The International Journal of Psycho-Analysis* 99(3): 555–568.

Stocker, Paul. 2019. *The Great Replacement Theory: A Historical Perspective.* September 19. https://www.opendemocracy.net/en/countering-radical-right/great-replacement-theory-historical-perspective/.

Summers, John H. 2005. *Why Do Historians Ignore Noam Chomsky.* January 6. Accessed April 29, 2021. https://historynewsnetwork.org/article/9538.

Tarrant, Brenton Harrison. 2016. *Terrorism Attacks.* February. Accessed May 14, 2021. https://ash.harvard.edu/terrorism-attacks.

———. n.d. "The Great Replacement." Accessed November 8, 2019. https://img-prod.ilfoglio.it/userUpload/The_Great_Replacementconvertito.pdf.

The Guardian. 2016. *Professor: Flight Was Delayed Because My Equations Raised Terror Fears.* May 7. Accessed August 30, 2021. https://www.theguardian.com/us-news/2016/may/07/professor-flight-delay-terrorism-equation-american-airlines.

———. n.d. *The Most Controversial Memes of All Times.* Accessed September 27, 2021. https://www.youtube.com/watch?v=4PGs-gJMvQI.

Thomas, B. Stephen, and C. Sandra Quinn. 2001. *Presidential Apology for the Study at Tuskegee.* August 17. Accessed May 27, 2021. https://www.britannica.com/topic/Presidential-Apology-for-the-Study-at-Tuskegee-1369625.

Tobias, Glen A., and Abraham H. Foxman. 2003. "Unraveling Anti-Semitic 9/11 Conspiracy Theories." *Anti-Defamation League.* Accessed November 11, 2021. https://www.adl.org/sites/default/files/documents/assets/pdf/combating-hate/anti-semitic-9-11-conspiracy-theories.pdf.

Torday, Daniel. 2020. *The Incoherence of Hate: Reading the Protocols of the Elders of Zion.* August 27. Accessed October 4, 2021. https://lithub.com/the-incoherence-of-hate-reading-the-protocols-of-the-elders-of-zion/.

Turner, Victor. 1974. *Drama, Fields and Metaphors: Symbolic Action in Human Society.* Ithaca: Cornell University Press.

———. n.d. *United States Cuban Refugee Program.* Accessed June 9, 2021. https://atom.library.miami.edu/united-states-cuban-refugee-program .

Uscinski, E. Joseph. 2019. *Conspiracy Theories and the People Who Believe Them.* Kindle Edition. London: Oxford University Press.

Uscinski, E. Joseph, and M. Joseph Parent. 2014. *American Conspiracy Theories.* Oxford: Oxford University Press.

———. n.d. *Violence and Socioeconomic Status.* Accessed November 24, 2021. https://www.apa.org/pi/ses/resources/publications/factsheet-violence.pdf.

Volpicelli, Gian M. 2021. *Telegram Is Becoming a Cesspool of Anti-Semitic Content*. October 13. Accessed December 7, 2021. https://www.wired.com/story/telegram -becoming-cesspit-antisemitic-content.

Wade, Nicholas. 2021. *The Origin of COVID: Did People or Nature Open Pandora's Box at Wuhan?* May 5. Accessed May 21, 2021. https://thebulletin.org/2021/05/ the-origin-of-covid-did-people-or-nature-open-pandoras-box-at-wuhan/.

Walker, Jesse. 2017. *The Age of Frank Gaffney*. March 21. https://reason.com/2017 /03/21/gaffney/.

Wan, William, Annie Gowen, and Tim Craig. 2018. *Pittsburgh Shooting Suspect Left Fleeting Impression in Neighborhoods He Lived in for Decades*. October 31. Accessed November 11, 2019. https://www.washingtonpost.com/national/ pittsburgh-shooting-suspect-left-fleeting-impression-in-neighborhoods-he-lived -in-for-decades/2018/10/31/90e1250c-dd44-11e8-b732-3c72cbf131f2_story .html.

Warzel, Charlie. 2019. *The 'Gamification' of Domestic Terrorism Online*. August 4. Accessed November 14, 2019. https://www.pbs.org/newshour/show/the -gamification-of-domestic-terrorism-online.

Weber, Max. 1958. "Science as a Vocation." In *From Max Weber: Essays in Sociology*, edited by H. H. Gerth and Wright C. Mills, 129–156. New York: Oxford University Press.

Webman, Esther, ed. 2011. *The Global Impact of the Protocols of the Elders of Zion: A Century-Old Myth*. Kindle Edition. New York: Routledge.

Weil, Julie Zauzmer. 2019. *The Alleged Synagogue Shooter Was a Churchgoer Who Talked Christian Theology, Raising Tough Questions for Evangelical Pastors*. May 1. Accessed November 26, 2021.

Weiner, Alyssa. 2020. "Global Trends in Conspiracy Theories Linking Jews with Coronavirus." *AJC (American Jewish Community Newsletter)*. May 1. Accessed September 6, 2022. https://www.ajc.org/news/global-trends-in-conspiracy -theories-linking-jews-with-coronavirus.

Wells, Georgia, and Ian Lovett. 2019. *"So What's His Kill Count?" The Toxic Online World Where Mass Shooters Thrive*. September 14. Accessed November 14, 2019. https://www.wsj.com/articles/inside-the-toxic-online-world-where -mass-shooters-thrive-11567608631.

White, Kesa. 2021. *Why the Oklahoma Bombing Continues to Cast a Shadow Over America*. August 12. Accessed August 14, 2021. https://www.radiofree.org/2021 /08/12/why-the-oklahoma-bombing-continues-to-cast-a-shadow-over-america/.

———. 2019. *Why Countering Violent Extremism Programs Are Bad Policy*. September 9. Accessed June 15, 2021. https://www.brennancenter.org/our-work /research-reports/why-countering-violent-extremism-programs-are-bad-policy.

Wilson, Jason. 2019. *White Supremacist Richard Spencer Makes Racist Slurs on Tape Leaked by Rival*. November 4. Accessed April 22, 2021. https://www .theguardian.com/world/2019/nov/04/white-supremacist-richard-spencer-racist -slurs-tape-milo-yiannopoulos.

Wood, Graeme. 2017. *His Kampf*. June 6. Accessed March 28, 2021. https://www .theatlantic.com/magazine/archive/2017/06/his-kampf/524505/.

Ye'Or, Bat. 2005. *The Euro-Arab Axis*. Vancouver: Fairleigh Dickinson University Press.

Zia-Ebrahimi, Reza. 2007. *There Is no Islamophobic Elephant in This Room: A Reflection on Houellebecq's Submission and Its Reception*. Accessed November 3, 2021. https://www.criticalmuslimstudies.co.uk/there-is-no-islamophobic-elephant -in-this-room-a-reflection-on-houellebecqs-submission-and-its-reception/.

Zimmerman, Moshe. 1986. *Wilhelm Marr: The Patriarch of Anti-Semitism*. New York: Oxford University Press.

Index

For Product Safety Concerns and Information please contact our EU
representative GPSR@taylorandfrancis.com
Taylor & Francis Verlag GmbH, Kaufingerstraße 24, 80331 München, Germany